HAUNTED
ADIRONDACKS

DENNIS WEBSTER

Haunted
America

Published by Haunted America
A Division of The History Press
Charleston, SC
www.historypress.com

First published 2021

Manufactured in the United States

ISBN 9781467149600

Library of Congress Control Number: 2021941045

This book is dedicated to two amazing women who were in my life before they passed away: my sweet and wonderful mother, Charlene Gifford Evans-Webster, and my beloved cousin Evelyn Webster. They were the first readers of every book I'd written. This tome is the first one I have written without their sage advice. I have felt their spirits around me, and I'm sure they checked over my shoulder as I sat in solitude and typed away. Charlene and Evie smiled and laughed every day. I love them and miss them.

CONTENTS

CONTENTS

FOREWORD

BY BERNADETTE PECK

I have spent the majority of my life seeing ghosts, communicating with them and making my passion and pursuit the seeking of a connection of my earthbound body to that of the spirits of the afterlife. It's been a strange and interesting paranormal thrill ride. I have the gift of sight and began seeing ghosts when I was a young girl and a ghost lady in red with raven hair would visit me. This journey of the haunted, the mysterious, the paranormal world of ghosts has been my life's passion. I have over sixty years of interaction with entities from another realm. I have theories on what ghosts are based on my life investigating haunted houses, cemeteries, asylums and historic battlefields. Ghosts are disembodied souls that can be seen and felt, either in solid form or in sensory form. They come for many reasons, some of which are to take care of unfinished business, deliver vital information, to protect loved ones or to reenact death. The afterlife can be heaven, and it can be hell, but the dead can operate and exist in between these two absolute realms, where the dead can retain their emotions and intelligence and have the ability to interact with the living.

I have walked among the most haunted locations in the world and count many among the inner blue line of the Adirondacks. The paranormal are amplified and reach super spooky heights within this region. The Adirondacks serve as a special hosting place for ghosts. The Adirondack Mountains have many rivers and lakes and are the dwelling places of ghosts and spirits of the dead. Water is a great conductor of energy, and of course, spirits are made up of energy. Our fragile earthbound flesh shells are merely bindings that

Bernadette Peck, a long-standing leader in the field of the paranormal and the founder and lead investigator of the Ghost Seekers of Central New York. *Photograph by Marrone Photography.*

hold our soul energy in place. On death, the flesh decays, but the soul stays. The Adirondack waterways hold the ghosts in place. The beauty within the blue line attracts the spirits who wish to retain their happy emotions. The clean and crisp mountain air that invigorates the living becomes desirable to the dead. There's been death and sadness, yet hope, fun and love in the Adirondacks. From Saranac Lake to Big Moose, I have been among the ghosts of the Adirondacks, and I understand, sympathize and smile, for what other place on the planet Earth would a ghost rather be?

AUTHOR'S NOTE ON THE PARANORMAL

I'm not your typical writer of ghost books. I'm a paranormal investigator, a ghost hunter, an empath, a disciple of Yoga Nidra and a chronicler of history, murders, ghosts and asylums. I'm an interdimensional jack of all trades, especially in my writing. The ghost stories you will read in this book are the result of my commitment and involvement with every place I've either visited, toured, guided or ghost hunted. I'm a believer in the afterlife and the realm of the dead. I have seen shadow people peeking around corners, witnessed curious ghosts staring me down in dusty attics, had a female entity rub me down during a séance and have had the grim reaper hovering over my bed during the witching hour, and I have lived through it all—at least as of the writing of this book. I started my journey in the world of the paranormal by being a skeptical writer whose scribe curiousness led me to write the book *Haunted Mohawk Valley*. This is when the Ghost Seekers of Central New York and acclaimed ghost hunter, leader and founder of the seekers, Bernadette Peck, let me shadow them on a paranormal investigation. I also had the privilege of shadowing and consulting with Damon Jacobs and his crack ghost squad: the Adirondack Park Paranormal Society (APPS). I took my experiences and founded my own team, the Fort Schuyler Paranormal Society (FSPS), along with medium/empath Sandy Silverstein and technical director Dave Silverstein. Along the way, I went from a skeptical observer to a participating believer. This curious paranormal journey opened up my third eye, and I have been able to experience things from the darker realm of the afterlife. I have come to the conclusion that ghosts are real. It's acceptable to embrace the dark, the unknown, the shadow people in the attic watching you. There's nothing to fear, so embrace these Adirondack locations, hunt your own ghosts and read these tales of the spooky with the lights on. The ghosts won't eat your souls for dinner, nor shall they haunt you—much.

MEMORIAL

Helen Clausen was an original member of the Ghost Seekers of Central New York and was a gifted person with the ability to see and communicate with spirits. Her dedication to the craft of paranormal research was a labor of love and curiosity. Her passing has left a large hole in the hearts of the seekers and the paranormal community. We miss you, Helen, and we shall see you again when we complete our journey on this spinning ball of mud and enter the spiritual realm.

Helen Clausen, a beloved member from the Ghost Seekers of Central New York. *Photograph by Marrone Photography.*

ACKNOWLEDGEMENTS

I 'd like to thank those who assisted in the development of this book: the Ghost Seekers of Central New York, Adirondack Park Paranormal Society (APPS), the Fort Schuyler Paranormal Society, Destiny Allen, Paul Allen, Josh Aust, Jim Bankich, Courtney Bastian, Mike Beck, Vicky Beck, Shawnee Black, Len Bragg, Richard Brewer, Liz Bridgman, Marcy Brunet, John Bruno, Ming Chen, Jennifer Coriale, Steve Dayter, Daniel DelGaudio, Bobbi DeLucia, Ann Marie Farrell, Aymee-Lynn "Alf" Fisk, Nicole M.G. Fleming, Erica Frick, Jeff Gee, Frank Giotto, Susan Murphy Goff, Carol Greenough, Laina Hamilton, Damon Jacobs, Michelle LeBlanc-Blair, Kate Lewis, Paranormal Ed Livingston, Kelly Martin, Captain Tom Mason, Sherry Matthews, R. Paul McCarty, Miranda Merrill, Matheau Morgan, Christy Nier, Cheryl Osterhout-Dayter, Joe Ostrander, Vida Pacheco, Sandy Pascucci, Bernadette Peck, David Peck, Moira Remington-Smith, Matt Rothwell, Kristy Rubyor, Heidi Schuller, Tyler Schuller, Dave Silverstein, Sandy Silverstein, Brendan Simons, Paul Stillman, Michael Takach, Stacia Takach, Jessica Trombley, Aaron Weaver, Anne Weaver, Mark Webster, Brett Williamson, Sarah Williamson and Josh Wingler.

The Adirondack Park Paranormal Society (APPS) was instrumental in the creation of this book; they conducted investigations and gave sage paranormal advice.

The Adirondack Park Paranormal Society (APPS) inside the haunted Hotel Saranac. *Author's collection.*

The Fort Schuyler Paranormal Society. *Photograph by Dave Silverstein.*

The Ghost Seekers of Central New York. *Author's collection.*

The Ghost Seekers of Central New York conducted many of the investigations featured in this book and brought forth the spirits that are captured in this tome.

The Fort Schuyler Paranormal Society (FSPS) assisted in the creation of this book and chose the haunted locations to visit and explore.

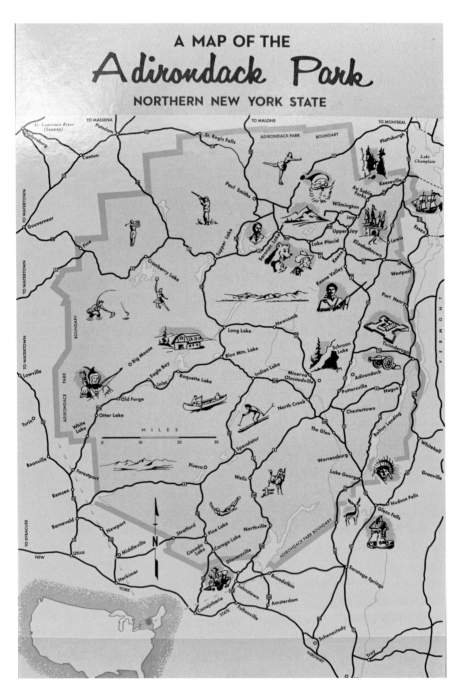

The Adirondack Park was established 1892 and comprises 102 towns and villages and 9,375 square miles. *Author's collection.*

THE ADIRONDACKS

The Adirondack Mountains are located in the northeastern part of New York State and were formed a billion years ago by a combination of erosion and glaciation. The topography of the Adirondacks is circular in area; they are domelike in appearance and cover over 9,000 square miles. It's been referred to as a new mountain range made up of old rocks. There are hundreds of peaks, with more than 40 soaring to heights over 4,000 feet, with the tallest peak located in New York State: Mount Marcy at 5,344 feet. The formulation of the Adirondacks make it a one-of-a-kind mountain range. As the glaciers from the last ice age receded, the range was left covered with lakes, streams, ponds, waterfalls, rivers, creeks, gorges and swampy bogs. There are over 2,300 lakes and ponds in the Adirondacks. The mountains are covered with pine, hemlock and spruce forests that are teeming with black bears and white-tailed deer, among many other animal species. The name *Adirondack* was derived from an Iroquois word meaning "eater of tree bark." The Adirondack Mountains are sparsely populated, and even to this day, there are many cellphone dead spots. They can be dangerous to hikers and campers who are not properly prepared to enter the range. The New York state legislature created the Adirondack Park in order to preserve and protect the mountain range; it is larger in area than the state of Vermont. It's no wonder that ghosts abound within the beauty of this alluring collective of mountains. Perhaps the spirits long to stay within the simple beauty of the Adirondacks.

HAUNTED LOCATIONS

T he following haunts are within the blue line of the Adirondack Mountains and cover all sections. These haunted locations are host to some of the scariest, strangest and saddest haunts you'll find anywhere in the United States. I challenge you, the reader, to visit every haunted location I visited and wrote about in this book. If you do, I'll list you in the paranormal club I dubbed the "ADK Haunted 25," and if you're a super ghost hunter and paranormal curiosity seeker, then go for the "best of the rest" haunted locations listed at the end of this book, along with a Bigfoot hunt in Whitehall or the Adirondack town of Ohio. I wish you luck in visiting these locations; perhaps you'll meet some of these ghosts, phantoms and a Bigfoot up close and personal. Be sure to tell them Dennis Webster said hello.

Dr. Trudeau's Adirondack Cottage Tuberculosis Sanitorium Saranac Lake

On the side of a steep hill, just outside of the town of Saranac Lake, sits a bundle of haunted buildings that, long ago, hosted people from all over the United States who had been afflicted with the deadly disease of tuberculosis (TB). The Adirondack Cottage Tuberculosis Sanitarium operated from 1884 to 1954 and was founded and run by Dr. Edward

Livingston Trudeau. People from all over the United States sought the fresh air of the Adirondacks to cure their debilitating lung disease, and many passed away, leaving their spirits behind. They were brought in by train to the Union Train Depot and then transported by horse and carriage up the hill to the beautiful mountain view and cool Adirondack air. Over fifty buildings were constructed on the sprawling hillside campus next to Saranac Lake. The James Staff Building, Dodd Building, Animal House and the Workshop are the epicenters of hauntings, with ghosts walking the halls, appearing to the living and slamming doors. The campus was owned by the American Management Association (AMA) for many years, but a sale to private owners allowed the Adirondack Park Paranormal Society (APPS) crew to spend four nights there, investigating the multitude of haunted buildings

Dr. Edward Livingston Trudeau (1848–1915) learned of Dr. Hermann Brehmer, who had successfully treated TB patients in Prussia by exposing them to cool, clear mountain air. He decided to go to the Adirondacks to replicate this methodology, and he founded the Saranac Laboratory for the study of tuberculosis, the first of its kind in the United States. Dr. Trudeau would give his life to his research, as he was diagnosed with tuberculosis in 1873 and lingered and suffered for decades before succumbing to the disease. He's been recognized as

Top: Dr. Edward Livingston Trudeau, who lost his life to tuberculosis while seeking a cure. *Author's collection.*

Bottom: A ghostly homunculus standing in a doorway of the James Building. *Photograph by Mark Webster.*

a pioneer in the world of medicine pre-antibiotics. Tuberculosis was a very painful and horrific disease of the lungs that you'd catch from inhaling air droplets from an infected person sneezing. A person with TB would cough up blood and have chills, night sweats, massive weight loss and loss of appetite and strength. There were hundreds of tragic and painful deaths from tuberculosis at the sanitarium, and they flooded the buildings and grounds with sad souls of the dead who took their pain and sorrow into the next realm. It was in this somber spiritual atmosphere that the APPS spent four nights, hunting ghosts and looking to connect with these poor departed souls. On two of these nights, APPS hosted a sister paranormal team, the Ghost Seekers of Central New York, so they could help investigate the massive buildings.

The James Building, where the doctors resided while treating tuberculosis. *Author's collection.*

The Adirondack Park Paranormal Society was founded by paranormal investigators Damon Jacobs, Sue Goff and Ann Farrell, with Jessica Trombley, Aymee-Lynee Fisk and Paul Allen providing ghost hunting support. The investigation was conducted by APPS over four chilly November nights, including two overnight hunts with the Ghost Seekers of Central New York. The Ghost Seekers were led by Bernadette Peck, along with her support team of paranormal investigators, Ed Livingston, Len Bragg, David Peck, Mark Webster, Liz Bridgman, Josh Aust and Dennis Webster. The groups used every kind of equipment they had in the field, including dowsing rods, laser grids, spirit boxes, EMF detectors and more. The campus was large, with dozens of buildings, so APPS narrowed their hunt down to the ones that were safe to be in and had past paranormal activity—they also considered the nature of the things that went on in these buildings. The buildings selected were the James Staff Building, Dodd Building, Animal House and Workshop. The command center/ghost central was based in the auditorium. Dr. Trudeau's Tuberculosis Sanitorium had never been ghost hunted before, and by the time all was said and done, the teams would walk

The Dodd Building, which housed many tuberculosis patients. *Author's collection.*

away mentally drained and physically depleted due to the vast amount of sad and lost ghosts trapped in the place where their diseased lungs betrayed their mortal beings, thus leaving them as eternal wandering spirits.

The Dodd Building was a large structure, with multiple floors and dozens of rooms that had hosted patients long ago; but the spirits remain, as it was very active during the investigation. There was a shadow person darting across the first floor, near the stage area. Then the building became rather flat, without a lot of activity. This is common during ghost hunts; activity comes in waves and shuts down as quickly as it appears. The teams found an odd staircase hidden around a corner that brought them across a walkway to the building next door. As the ghost hunters were walking down the dark, narrow hallway, a large oak door slammed shut with such a force and noise that everyone jumped with shrieks. Yes, even ghost hunters can become frightened by angry entities. When the activity returned in the Dodd Building, doors kept opening and shutting with the assistance of ghostly hands that were captured on video. The group did a spirit box session on the second floor that produced incredible evidence. A spirit box is a device that searches FM radio waves and produces words and phrases. Most of it is

The Animal House, where spooky events shook the paranormal investigators to their spiritual cores. *Author's collection.*

gibberish, but when the ghosts use the spirit box to communicate, you'll get intelligent responses. Sue Goff was asking the questions, and the box said, "Suzy," along with other phrases that coincided with questions asked.

The Animal House building was a dank, dirty and sad place with peeling paint and industrial experimental décor that caused everyone to feel off-kilter, sad and drained of energy. During the pre-investigation walkthrough, the ghost hunters heard footsteps, and all of the equipment was drained. The atmosphere was heavy and creepy. Everyone left, and the front door was unlocked, but when everyone returned to investigate, it was suddenly locked. There was no one near the Animal House at the time, as the campus was closed to visitors. It was obvious something didn't want the paranormal investigators inside. Once the door was unlocked and everyone was inside, Josh got a massive headache and channeled the name of a young boy named Thomas. The spiritual lad said he had arrived by train at the Union Depot in Saranac Lake. He said that he had worked in Animal House and passed away there. Thomas was lonely and wanted to go home. He said he had been trapped in the Animal House a long time. It was a sad moment, and the team tried to move his spirit on to the next plane of existence, away from where he was trapped. Several of the team members got physically ill and overwhelmed by the sadness of the ghosts and had to leave. Sue Goff stated that nothing drained her like this building and the others on the campus. The campus was filled with the spirits of the tuberculosis patients, and they transferred their sadness to the living paranormal investigators.

The James Building produced some ghosts, but it mainly produced a photograph that one has to see to believe. This was the building that had housed the doctors and nurses who tried their best to cure those suffering with tuberculosis. The majority of these loving caretakers caught the disease and died from it. Two different investigators, Ann and Josh, put their hands on a door on the second floor and saw a female entity with curly hair. During an EVP in the area, Sue picked up a ghost saying, "Help me." This was an answer to an investigator asking, "Do you know you're dead?" The team got an off-putting feeling, and Mark captured an odd ghost with his camera. It was a small human figure, only a few feet tall. On further analysis, the team deemed the ghost was a homunculus. A homunculus is a fully formed small human created by alchemy; they were popular in the sixteenth century. This is one of the most odd and best paranormal photographs ever captured by the ghost hunters from both teams. Bernadette and Damon deemed it too sad, and the groups refused to go back in there. As the night was concluding and everyone was getting worn out, there were some ghost experiences that were still to happen.

The auditorium, where command and ghost central was located, had spirits interacting with individuals, even though it was filled with investigators, equipment strewn all about and all the lights on. One investigator witnessed an entity sitting in a chair in the middle of the room. Bernadette and Josh went into the basement and channeled a female murder victim. The last building the teams went to was the Workshop. When everyone was on the first floor, it was rather sterile, with not a lot happening, but once the group moved to the second floor, it got hostile. The teams encountered a religious man who was either a priest, deacon or preacher; he did not like having anyone in his space and was answering Paul as he conducted tests with the dowsing rods. The male ghost revealed that the Workshop had been a place where there were no smiles, a place where discipline was meted out, a place where the living suffered for their sins and where he wished to continue the punishment in the afterlife. Damon and Sue made the decision to evacuate and regroup at the command center.

The Adirondack Park Paranormal Society and the Ghost Seekers of Central New York agreed that Dr. Trudeau's Adirondack Cottage

Tuberculosis Sanitorium was the most draining and sad ghost hunting experience they'd ever had. It was not scary or insidious—just sad. The sadness was compounded by many spirits who had experienced a death of suffering and whose woes cry for all eternity. They latched onto the living energy of the team members and, like paranormal vampires, sucked the positive life essence from every team member. The teams gathered at the end and said a prayer of hope for the tuberculosis spirits—that they may find peace and health in the realm where they forever roam.

FORT WILLIAM HENRY
LAKE GEORGE

It's an honor to walk the holy land of patriotic sacrifice, especially when it hosted liberty and freedom. Fort William Henry sits on the southern bank of Lake George and was a British fort built in 1755. It was later destroyed by the French during the French and Indian War in 1757. It was reconstructed in 1955, based on the original British plans, and it sits primarily on the site of the original. It was christened Fort William Henry in honor of the grandsons of King George II. The British lost a battle to the French and Natives on August 9, 1757, and after the British withdrawal, the sick and wounded who were left behind were massacred, and the fort was burned to the ground by the Natives. The dead totaled, according to historians, between 200 and 1,500 soldiers and civilians. The reconstructed fort was built on the bodies of the brave and hosts ghosts hundreds of years later, with many tourists seeing and feeling the spirits. I bought my ticket for the tour, but being the infiltrator and ghost hunter that I am, I broke away from the large tour group and walked the fort by myself. I preferred to engage the ghosts solo.

The day was so sunny, and the sky was so blue that my eyes hurt from the glare of the wooden posts, and walking the shaded areas of Fort William Henry was mandatory for comfort. I was walking alone on the grounds and stopped a young man by the name of Mason Kladis, who said he was a reenactor at the fort and that he was pleased to speak to me about the ghosts. He said that people will smell bread baking, which is very normal when it comes to hauntings. The paranormal can produce familiar odors, whether it's perfume, tobacco or baking bread. Ghosts have been seen playing cards in the fort, and during the night, when there are no visitors, Mason said the reenactors have heard voices. He took me to the second floor of the fort, where there are bunks,

Hallowed ground inside of Fort William Henry. *Author's collection.*

and he told me, one night, when he was sleeping there, he heard footsteps and knocks from the room next door. He jumped from his bunk and opened the door, but no one was there. He told me the below-ground casemate area was the most haunted spot. I went to that area, and there were several steps where I was plunged into darkness. It took my eyes several minutes to adjust so I could make out the area. There were benches in the bunker and several displays of medical models. I sat on the bench and was writing in my journal when I saw Mason coming with another reenactor who introduced himself as Aron Connors, a medical historian at the fort who had ghost stories to tell me. He said he always feels a chilling breeze down in the casemate area, where it's not possible, and he said that he had seen the ghost of a little girl down there. She likes to sit on one of the benches. Many had seen her, so the staff now leaves a small vase with flowers for her. I looked over, and there were flowers out for the little girl's ghost. Aron told me that the grounds of the fort still held many buried bodies under six feet of packed sand and that the ghost of a Native had been seen walking the steps of the fort. I thanked Aron for sharing his experiences, and he and Mason left to get back to the tourists above. I was alone then, and I was writing in my journal. I sat on the bench that was

Above: A Fort William Henry guide points to where he was sleeping when he heard ghostly footsteps. *Author's collection.*

Right: The bench inside the haunted casemate area of Fort William Henry. *Author's collection.*

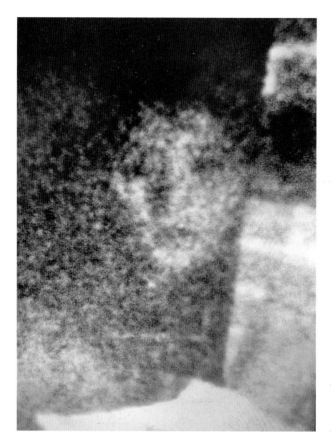

The little girl ghost of
Fort William Henry.
*Courtesy of Fort William
Henry.*

favored by the little girl's ghost when I suddenly felt a cold breeze. It startled me, and I stopped and looked around. There was nobody there, so I went back to writing. I again felt a breeze, so I stopped writing and said, "Are you the little girl? You can come sit by me. You have my permission. I don't mind." Nothing materialized, so I set my journal down, clasped my hands, closed my eyes and said, "What is your name?" I heard, "Abigail." So, I said, "Nice to meet you Abigail." As soon as I said this, I got ice cold on my right side, and I knew her ghost had come and sat next to me on the bench. I did not dare to open my eyes. I just sat with her ghost in silence for what seemed an eternity, but it was really only a minute before I became warm, and I knew she had gotten up and moved on. I opened my eyes, and I was all alone in the casemate. But I smiled, as Abigail had trusted me, and I could sense her joy and playfulness being confined within Fort William Henry. If you visit, be sure to bring a flower and sit on the bench in the casemate—her spirit just might say hello.

Old Fort House
Fort Edward

In the pursuit of ghosts and the paranormal, they sometimes find you or offer themselves in the most unexpected ways. I had been in Fort Edward to look at another haunted location, but I found it closed, and there was no one able to speak to me on the topic. I had to turn around to leave Fort Edward, so I pulled into a driveway and saw a very old and beautiful yellow colonial-era homestead. But it was what was out front that piqued my curiosity. It was a sign posted that said, "Ghost Tour tonight with Ben Franklin." I parked my truck and realized it was a historical place: the Old Fort House. I walked into the gift shop and purchased a ticket for the tour and met R. Paul McCarthy, the executive director, and he talked to me about the history of the home and mentioned that the gentleman giving the tour that night would be dressed as Ben Franklin. McCarthy said he was a rather talented man who was an empath, medium, shaman and exorcist. The man was Paul Stillman, a member of the Allegheny Seneca

The Old Fort House in all its haunted glory. *Author's collection.*

Nation. I was impressed and thrilled to be going back, as the history of the Old Fort House was important to the history of the United States. It was built in 1772 by Patrick Smyth from timbers salvaged from Fort Edward. The house had been used by the British and colonists during the Revolutionary War. It had also hosted James Madison and George Washington. The yellow mansion had hosted Solomon Northup between 1830 and 1834, when he wrote *12 Years a Slave*, one of the most important memoirs in the history of the United States, which was adapted as an Oscar-winning movie. Solomon had been a free man in New York State before he was taken down south and sold as an enslaved man. His memoir exposed the reality of those in slavery and rallied the North to abolish the practice. The Old Fort House was listed in the National Register of Historic Places in 1983. I was soon to experience an emotional connection to a ghost on the grounds of the haunted campus, as the Old Fort House also has several buildings that were relocated there, making it a spooky place to walk in the dark.

The ghost tour was about to start at dark, but I got there an hour early so I could walk the grounds and take in all the buildings and the grounds. The sun was setting, and night was creeping in as I walked around the buildings, admiring their historical aesthetics. I got near the greenhouse, and my entire body lit up; I felt a sadness, and my heart raced. My nose burned from an odor I couldn't identify. The structure looked newer, but there was something unsettling about that spot. After my walkthrough, I sat on a bench in front of the Old Fort House, and after a few minutes, Paul Stillman pulled up, got out of his car, dressed in colonial garb, and placed a Revolutionary War era–style hat on his head. He had a grand appearance and long gray hair pulled into a ponytail. I walked up to him to say hello, and he said, "There's something about you. May I read you?" I said OK, and he asked me to hold my hands out. He pinched them each with his thumb and pointer finger and looked into my eyes. I got an odd feeling that was like an electrical jolt, and my hands started to shake. He let go of me, smiled and said, "I thought so." I was rattled for a moment and sat quietly by myself as a few other people arrived to partake in the ghost tour. Darkness crept in, and we were about to start when I asked Paul about the location that I felt was haunted and had caused me sadness. He smiled and said, "You'll see."

The tour was well done, as Paul led the group from building to building, telling the history of each, but everyone nodded with admiration and respect when he pointed out the second-floor window where *12 Years a Slave* was

The greenhouse now sits on the spot of a tragedy that produced a sad entity. *Author's collection.*

A ghost tour of the Old Fort House by the spiritually connected shaman and exorcist Paul Stillman. *Author's collection.*

written by Solomon Northup. The tour had been going nicely, with eerie feelings felt by all and many photographs being taken, when a mist came off the river and crept across the moist grass. When we walked toward the greenhouse, I stopped and watched as Paul and the rest went over then came back. One lady on the tour captured what looked like a large spirit light in the location that had creeped me out. Paul went on to say that the spot had experienced a tragedy long ago, when a barn had been located there. Over one hundred years ago, a family was working in the barn, hoisting large bales of hay. While they were lifting the hay bales, the family's young son was walking through the barn. Suddenly, the rope broke, causing a hay bale to come crashing down on the boy, killing him instantly. The next day, the boy's grandparents, in their grief, burned the barn to the ground. Paul said, during certain nights, you can smell the burned embers, with many theorizing it is the anniversary of the boy's demise. I was stunned at this revelation, as the smell I had experienced in that spot had been that of a paranormal bouquet. I named the boy Samuel, as that was the name that had come to me. I thought being named might make the little boy's ghost feel better. I thanked Samuel for his visit. I walked the rest of the ghost tour in silence as I thought of the spirit of the little boy lost on that spot, and I hoped that, someday, he'd cross over to a place of happiness and peace. Paul took the group to the dark back lot, and everyone experienced a creep factor that was enhanced by his masterful storytelling and the history of this marvelous place. I left, looking one last time at the location of the greenhouse, and I said a prayer under my breath for the ghosts of the tragedy who were trapped. I prayed for Samuel.

WOODGATE FREE LIBRARY
WOODGATE

Driving north up Route 28, just as you cross the blue line into Adirondack Park, you come across the small town of Woodgate. To the left of the blinking light is a very small building next to the post office. The Woodgate Free Library is a small and inviting one-story structure that is packed to the walls with ghosts and paranormal activity. The director of the library, Sandy Pascucci, has had many haunted experiences in the little building that was built in 1880 and started out as a schoolhouse. Back then, the town was called White Lake Corners. The ghost that is seen and felt most often

The Woodgate Free Library. *Author's collection.*

there is a young girl entity that has been identified from a class photograph dated 1915. Clara Hurlburt was her name, and she was seen and felt when medium Bobbi DeLucia walked through on her spiritual library quest. By 1931, there was a new schoolhouse down the road, and the little one became the library, but Clara's ghost remained. There were other spirits around to complement the ghostly student. There had been paranormal ghost hunts conducted in the library, as well as Bobbi's medium walkthrough, and all yielded results. The best investigation would be the last at the library, but it was done in the form of a nineteenth-century séance.

Sandy asked the Ghost Seekers of Central New York to come and meet her and consider an investigation. I drove up there on a hot and humid Adirondack summer day with my brother Mark Webster. The library was small, but we could feel the heaviness as soon as we crossed the threshold. We went back to Bernadette Peck, the lead investigator, founder and ghost hunter of Ghost Seekers of Central New York with over forty years of experience in the world of paranormal phenomenon. She decided it would be best to perform a séance instead of a full-blown investigation. Her ghostly instincts are usually right on the money. It would prove to be a wise decision, as the ghost seekers would experience a thrilling and frightening interaction in the midnight darkness of the library. The one-story, two-room library had been investigated by other ghost groups that had found all sorts of spirits and entities, but this was the first time a séance was held in the library. It's a ritual that must be performed with delicacy, accuracy and respect for those who are dead.

Sandy told the group about the books that had been thrown from the shelves many times by mischievous ghosts; most of the time it was a couple of large cookbooks, but she didn't say what the other large volume had been. She asked if the ghost seekers might be able to identify the third ghost-thrown title. When the group walked in, it was composed of Bernadette Peck, David Peck, Josh Aust, Paranormal Ed Livingston, Len Bragg, Mark Webster and yours truly. Mark is the quiet one of the group, and this was his first official ghost investigation. He walked the through thousands of book titles in the library and picked out a large blue book that was a biography on Harry Truman; Sandy was astounded and declared that it, indeed, was the other book being thrown by the ghost. The séance was set up in the traditional fashion, with a Saint David candle in the middle of the table, unlit sage in case we needed to cleanse the area, all of the ghost handheld devices, digital recorders and a video camera on a tripod. The darkness was as thick as squid ink outside, and the team sat at the table, lit the candle, held hands and recited an opening prayer. The séance is performed by keeping your hands locked together the entire time, as the group uses its energy to make a ghost appear. It didn't take long for the spirits to engage, and Len had something talking right behind him. Sandy, Helen and Bernadette had something breathing on their necks, and Josh's empathic mental gifts were on fire. I had brought along my rosary beads and had them wrapped around my right hand—the hand I had interlocked with my brother's. Mark said he felt my hand vibrating and rattling then felt the rosary beads start to swing back and forth from a ghost slapping them. The team could hear footsteps, and Bernadette had a ghost talking gibberish right behind her. The séance lasted for only forty-five minutes, as the body and spirit of the group tired and became drained. The event takes a toll on the mind, body and spirit when there are ghosts circling and interacting. The ghost seekers ended the séance, broke the chain and released the spirits to go back to the realm of the ones who have passed away.

There was a lot more than just the ghost of the little girl Clara present, and the team wondered if there was a portal in the library. It was at this point that the group discovered something disturbing and shocking. The group looked at some bookcases that looked different from all the rest in the library. There was a "Property of Utica State Hospital" sticker on them. The wooden bookcases had been donated and came from Old Main, the lunatic asylum in Utica, New York. Old Main is one of the most haunted asylums in America and experienced 150 years of sadness. Objects can have ghosts attached to them, and the spirits of the long-suffering asylum patients most certainly could be behind some of the haunted shenanigans at the Woodgate Public Library. If you stop at the Woodgate Free Library, be sure to hold the Truman book, smile and say hello to the little girl ghost Clara and say a prayer for the tormented souls trapped and attached to the asylum bookcases. Perhaps your prayers can help move them along to another dimension of peace and tranquility.

Medium Bobbi DeLucia, Woodgate Free Library Walkthrough and Adirondack Ghost Analysis

I know medium Bobbi DeLucia, and she is the best viewer of spirits I have ever met. I knew she had performed a walkthrough of the Woodgate Free Library, and I asked her to describe her experience. I then asked her to please give you, dear reader, her viewpoint and theory on ghosts in the Adirondacks. The following are her words:

> *Webster's Dictionary defines an impression as an idea, feeling or opinion about something or someone, formed without conscious thought or on the basis of little evidence. In stating that, my first impression of the public library in Woodgate was that it was "busy." That in and of itself would not be odd had it not been for the fact I was visiting at ten o'clock in the evening, and by busy, I meant ghostly activity. Immediately upon exiting my vehicle, there was a predominantly male presence beckoning me to enter the building, out of the cold. Walking into the building was like walking into an only milder version of the parking lot, the energy in the building creating an equally chilly reception. Without removing my jacket, I followed the male energy to the far back office, although I was not invited to enter the room. Standing outside of the office, the energy was stronger, and I shivered while watching everyone around me appeared comfortably warm. There were myriad noises, from the rustling of pages, to the shuffling of feet and giggling of young children. To the shocked stares of those with me, I was becoming intolerant to the cold and loudly stated that the entities needed to step away from me, at which point, several books fell to the floor. I'd made it a point to pull our guide aside and discuss with her at length the male energy I'd felt from the moment I arrived, as he had made it quite clear to me that they knew one another. She had validated that, yes, a man had*

worked there that she had known very well, who did, in fact, use the office I had been led to. We discussed his passing, the things he had done for the community in which he lived and his feelings about the progress since his passing. Through this validation, the room seemed to warm slightly as his mood shifted. Regardless of this, until we left, we continued to see small light anomalies, hear shuffling and, at one point, I thought I had heard the muffled sounds of music.

What is it that draws the living and the dead to the wonders of the Adirondacks? Why do we stay? Is it the hauntingly mournful wails of the loon; opulent bodies of water surrounded by eerie, vast woodlands; or something else altogether? Spirits of cultures long past roam those woodlands, buildings having housed more history than most books still standing strong and proud as a testament to their trials.

Having lived in the Adirondacks for more than half of my life, as a medium, I can tell you that it is all of this and perhaps more. I've found that the energizing properties of the running streams cause peaks in my abilities; in contrast, the magnetic pull from the land itself grounds me. Long walks on nearly silent wooded trails have heightened every sixth sense I've taken years to develop. When you are looking for adventures of the spiritual [paranormal] kind, hike the woods, take in the water and scenery. Prepare yourself for more than you had ever bargained for, knowing you will never be walking alone.

VAN AUKEN'S INNE
THENDARA

Van Auken's Inne is a haunted bar, restaurant and hotel right next to the tracks of the Adirondack Scenic Railroad in the town of Thendara. Just looking at Van Auken's Inne from the train station gives one a sense of awe and wonderment, and there are ghosts inside, waiting to meet and greet the living. The town of Thendara is right next to Old Forge and, at one time, was the local hub of business in that region. The original name of the town was Fulton Chain. The area first started to develop because of its vast abundance of logs and proximity to the sawmill and train that ran right through the heart of Fulton Chain. It was right next to the Fulton Chain Railroad Station, and a large hotel, Mack's Hotel, was built in 1894 by Cornelius Mack. This was the place where the hardworking lumberjacks

Charlie the ghost can be seen on the far right in all white at the Van Auken's Inne. *Courtesy of Van Aukin's Inne.*

The modern look of the popular Van Auken's Inne. *Author's collection.*

would stay while working lengthy hours cutting, stacking and moving logs and wood. This was a very dangerous but necessary occupation in a growing United States. It was in Mack's Hotel where the blue-collar Adirondack spirit was alive and where it still roams to this day. In 1895, the hotel was sold to John J. Wakely, who renamed it the Wakely Hotel. He would not own it long, as the Tennis brothers would buy it and move it seventy-five feet away from the tracks in 1904. This was done because its proximity to the tracks was causing an increased risk of fire. The smoke that was being emitted from the Adirondack Railroad engines could throw sparks onto the wood building and cause a deadly fire. Eventually, the three-story hotel was renamed the Van Auken Inne. The grand Victorian structure has entertained visitors to the Adirondacks for many decades. The Van Auken Inne has long been rumored to be haunted, and all one needs to do is stop in and ask any staff person, as the spirits roam the hotel hallways and wander through the kitchen and bar. The owners, Suzan and Jim Moore, allowed the Ghost Seekers of Central New York to come in and conduct a paranormal investigation to determine if the legendary haunted Van Auken Inne lived up to its haunted reputation.

The ghost hunt was conducted on May 16, 2015. It was a sunny and warm day, with the scent of the pines wafting across the front porch. The bar was open to the public, but the haunted hotel area was closed. There was revelry, fun and music in the bar, and that ended up bringing out the spirits. The ghost seekers, led by Bernadette Peck, were greeted by the very friendly owner Jim, who accompanied the team down to the speakeasy in the basement that had been under construction and was not yet open to the public. An employee who also came along said she was down there alone when a ghost whispered "hello" in her ear, causing her to flee back up the stairs. On the first floor, it had been reported that a Santa Clause decoration with a motion detector kept going off, as the ghosts kept playing with it. Knickknacks and random items would move from a poltergeist, causing a bartender to flee. The employee never came back. The employees also declared that radios turn on and off all by themselves. Many had reported seeing a male ghost in a white coat that they called Charlie. There is an old black-and-white photograph of Van Auken's Inne from the early twentieth century. It shows a row of people standing on the front porch. You can make out all of the faces of except that of the man in white on the very end. Everyone claims that was Charlie when he was alive. It's spooky seeing a ghost standing on a porch with the living. Current employees have also claimed that rooms 8, 9 and 12 of the hotel are haunted, as there had been many sightings, and an employee was choked by a ghost in room 12. The stairwell by the kitchen has also had a ghost walking up and down it that had been seen by many employees.

The Ghost Seekers of Central New York conducted the investigation with one team in the basement and one team upstairs in the hotel. The entire group in the basement saw a shadow person walking where the speakeasy bar was being constructed. I was down in the basement, along with Bernadette Peck and the team's empath, Josh Aust. Josh got a headache right away, then we channeled the spirit of a nun. Bernadette got the name Sarah from the lonely nun ghost. There were voices from the other side talking to us, and we felt compelled to go to the root cellar, where we saw the spirit of a little boy hiding in the corner. Josh got the name Matthew from the little boy ghost and asked him to come closer. I felt this little entity brush against me, causing massive goosebumps all over my body, as he walked right up to Bernadette and Josh. The meters and flashlight were sitting on a wooden barrel next to them, and the devices blasted; the flashlight turned on as if Matthew was curious, and he attempted to play with the devices.

Ghost Seekers David Peck, Paranormal Ed Livingston, Helen Clausen and Joe Ostrander reported hearing voices and witnessing ghostly movements up in the rooms. The team went up into room 12 and didn't experience much, but rooms 8 and 9 were teeming with paranormal activity. Room 8 had air that was tough to breathe, and it had a feeling of darkness and heaviness. The group picked up what they felt was the ghost of a man who had committed suicide in the room and was now hanging for all eternity in the bathroom. Bernadette went in by herself, sat in the tub and felt kinetic electricity throughout her body. The group channeled and picked up the spirit of Charlie, who was upbeat and positive, the polar opposite of the suicide entity. Charlie was happy to spend his time at Van Auken's Inne. All night long, the ghost seekers encountered very active ghosts, with Helen feeling the presence of the boy, Matthew, who rubbed up against her leg. Everyone experienced cold chills, and it was determined by the professional ghost hunters that Van Auken's Inne was a very haunted place. They also confirmed that Charlie the ghost does, indeed, walk the halls and loves being dead in the Adirondack jewel of Thendara. If you are brave, then stay in rooms 8, 9 or 12.

GOODSELL MUSEUM
OLD FORGE

Right in the middle of Old Forge is a cute little red house that was, at one time, the loving home of the Goodsell family. It now belongs to the Town of Webb Historical Society and is called the Goodsell Museum. There's more than just history on display in this place; there are ghosts. One is that of the former living resident Tena Goodsell. Tena's father, George Goodsell, built the charming red-and-white Victorian house in 1899. It's described as "a two-story, gable-fronted, Victorian vernacular frame dwelling." Tena was seen looking out of the third-story window by a passerby as they strolled down the sidewalk out front. When she was alive, Tema was known to be shy and would stand on her front porch and observe the people walking past. It seems her ghost continues this in the afterlife. George's son Robert Goodsell lived his entire life in the home, remained a lifelong bachelor and passed away in 1994 after a life of one hundred years. Tena also lived a long life and passed away at the age of ninety-two. The Goodsell family left their beloved home to the Town of Webb Historical Society, and it was lovingly named the Goodsell Museum. The red landmark is listed in the New York State and National Register of Historic Places and packs in tourists and locals the year round. Some have encountered the ghosts. It seems that the living and the dead love the Goodsell Museum. Kate Lewis is the director of the Goodsell Museum, and Kristy Rubyor is the assistant; they are both more than happy to discuss the haunted icon nestled in the middle of Old Forge.

They tell stories of the ghosts, including a the second-floor interaction one had with a couple visitors. A man and his young daughter were walking through the museum. The items on display had been changed, and there was a second-floor room that had old doctor's equipment on display. Kate Lewis said that the visitors were up there alone and that the father had walked out of this room and left his young daughter looking at the items. She was alone in the room, yet when he was in the hall, he could hear a man's voice coming from within. His young daughter walked out, and when he asked who she was talking to, she replied, "A nice old man." The father walked right in, but there was nobody there. Kate had also spoken about doors opening on their own and footsteps heard throughout the museum. Kate asked the Ghost Seekers of Central New York to conduct a spiritual investigation in the museum and the carriage barn. The group was more than happy to oblige. I visited Kate with Bernadette Peck on a

The historically haunted Goodsell Museum in Old Forge. *Courtesy of the Town of Webb Historical Association.*

spring day in 2014. During our preliminary walkthrough, we could feel the spiritual energy in the air, and Bernadette felt it was prime to be hunted for ghosts. I was in a second-floor storage room, just looking around, when a stack of papers flew off a shelf and hit me in the chest. The seekers returned, investigated and got direct interaction with entities, ghosts and shadow people. The paranormal investigative team included Bernadette

Tena Goodsell. *Courtesy of the Town of Webb Historical Association.*

Peck, David Peck, Joe Ostrander, Josh Aust, Len Bragg, psychic Irene Crewell, Paranormal Ed Livingston and me. It was a perfect night for ghosts, as the ink-black night was pierced by beams of illumination from the moon streaming through the museum windows. Kate Lewis was there, watching the monitors of the night vision cameras that were streaming back to the large flatscreen display at ghost central, located in the first-floor record room that hosted old newspapers and a large table where one could sit and conduct historical research. The investigation confirmed the haunting of the Goodsell Museum, as the team witnessed a shadow figure in the carriage barn, spidery ghost fingers streaming down their faces in the dark, footsteps on the first floor, knocks on demand, the smell of cherry pipe tobacco, steps in the second-floor donors' office display and the vision of Tena Goodsell. The scent of the tobacco had been the favorite of a long-dead caretaker. Smells can be sensed among paranormal hauntings. Ghosts hit all five of the human senses when they haunt.

The ghost of Tena was witnessed by four members of the team on two separate trips to the attic. The ghost would remain by the front window and peer at the investigators around storage shelves and bookshelves. This confirmed eyewitness accounts of her peering out the attic window, watching pedestrians go past. She didn't speak, but she did intelligently move closer to the group as they beckoned her to engage with the living. Recently, I stopped in to see Kate and Kristy and to see if anything haunted had happened recently, and they said they had experienced a great paranormal event. Kristy had closed all the interior doors to the Goodsell Museum and locked it up. She was the first person in early the next morning, and the playful spirits had opened all of the doors. In discussing the ghosts with Kate, she mentioned that the museum was bringing in different historical items and that ghosts could be coming along with the displayed pieces. It is true that ghosts can be attached to material items that they loved or were fond of in this realm and that they will go along to guard their earthly possessions. Perhaps they revel in mortals enjoying their former possessions. The Goodsell Museum is among the most haunted buildings in the Adirondacks, and it is certainly the most haunted building in Old Forge. So, the next time you're in the village, pay your admission and walk around, speaking to Tena—she just might appear to greet you.

Old Forge Hardware
Old Forge

When driving through the picturesque town of Old Forge, New York, you see a row of businesses, homes and camps, with one that is well known nationally: the Old Forge Hardware Store. The building hosts thousands of items from hammers and books to Adirondack-themed gifts. It's an overstuffed shoppers' delight that's as haunted as any building you will find. The spirit of the original owner, Moses Cohen, has been seen at night, walking the rows of his beloved store. Many locals who work nearby get off from work late at night and see Moses checking his inventory while walking by. The Old Forge Hardware Store has a long history, with Moses starting the business back in 1902, when he purchased a corner lot and built the

Moses Cohen, the original owner of the Old Forge Hardware Store. *Courtesy Old Forge Hardware.*

original structure. Tragedy would strike the store when it burned down in 1922, but Moses rebuilt it in 1923. The Old Forge Hardware Store served an important community need back in the days when traveling the Adirondacks was much more difficult in the winter months. Locals needed their sundries and goods to conduct business and stay alive in the harsh months. His soul connected to his beloved business, so it's perfectly natural to think that his ghost would come to our plane of existence to stroll and inspect the goods. The Old Forge Hardware Store is currently owned by Erica and Terry Murray, and it continues to thrive, serving and satisfying the public. During tourist season, one can hardly walk the aisles, as crowds clog every inch of the haunted structure. Erica invited the Ghost Seekers of Central New York to conduct a paranormal investigation during the summer of 2014. The team consisted of Bernadette Peck, David Peck, Psychic Irene Crewell, Helen Clausen, Len Bragg, Josh Aust and me. The night of the ghost hunt was a cliché dark and stormy night, yet the thunder and flashes of lightning off in the distance did electrify the team and brought forth a cornucopia of paranormal activity.

During the equipment setup, the team found a photograph negative on the floor in the back storage and inventory area. This area is not open to

The popular and iconic Old Forge Hardware Store. *Author's collection.*

the public and is very neat and orderly. David and I were running cable for the video camera and walked through, and there was nothing on the floor. But when we turned around, there it was, a photograph negative placed right in the middle of the floor. The picture was developed, but no one was able to identify the spooky-looking girls in the photograph that appeared to be from the 1940s. The ghosts were trying to send a message, and to this day, it has not been solved, with local historians and longtime Old Forge Hardware Store employees unable to identify the mystery girls.

As soon as the investigation started, Helen, Len and Josh encountered a spirit in the bookstore, where responses were given to questions and the team picked up a recording of talking and footsteps. Helen witnessed a dark shadow entity ducking and hiding behind the bookshelves. Helen described the entity as "not of this earth." At the same time, Bernadette, David, Irene and I witnessed a shadow person walking across the mezzanine section that is in the original part of the hardware store. The store was closed for the night, and Erica had locked the team inside, so there was no way it was a random shopper or employee. A paranormal hot spot was found when the team conducted an electronic voice phenomenon (EVP) session in the storage area, where the mystery ghost negative had been left.

The team heard footsteps and used a flashlight to ask the spirits to light it on being questioned. The intelligent ghost responded over and over again, and the team remained calm in its presence. It was very warm and humid in the room, yet the team suddenly became embraced by the other side, as a wave of cold air hit everyone and enveloped the group. The temperature became bone-chilling cold as the interactions with the spirits intensified. At this point, I felt a ghost brush up against my arm, and every hair on my body stood up—I was speechless. Bernadette came face to face with a dark shadow person that walked right past her. Could it have been Moses checking on his inventory?

There is no doubt that the Old Forge Hardware Store is very haunted and that the ghost of Moses Cohen walks through the merchandise every evening. The next time you're in the Old Forge Hardware Store, be sure to look for the ghosts in the mezzanine and the bookstore area. Ghosts long for the love of our world and miss the materialistic pleasures they left behind. There's not a better or more beautiful place for Moses to spend his afterlife than in the place he built and now lovingly watches from his spiritual realm.

THE WOODS INN
INLET

On the banks of Fourth Lake is a glorious hotel that is not only beautiful but also paranormally alluring and overstuffed with ghosts. The yellow-and-white exterior pops from within the trees nestled around the perimeter and is a glorious wonder from the water. The Woods Inn was built in 1894 and had originally been operated as the Hess Camp, named after its builder, Fred Hess. In the beginning, the camp delivered guests by steamboat. This mode of transportation also brought employees and operational sundries to the camp. The building was then sold to longtime manager Philo Wood, and he renamed it the Wood Hotel. From 1900 to 1920, he expanded the building and placed cottages and platforms for tents on the property. He proved to be a successful owner, with dozens of elite and famous guests who stayed for relaxation and fresh Adirondack air. In 1946, Bill Dunay purchased the hotel and ran it until he closed it in 1979, but he kept the tavern open and running until his death in 1989. The Woods Inn remained empty for many years until it was purchased in 2003 by Joedda McClain and Jay Latterman.

Above: The Woods Inn in all its haunted glory. *Author's collection.*

Right: Ectoplasm on the steps inside the Woods Inn. *Courtesy of the Woods Inn.*

They painstakingly renovated the hotel to its current beauty and reopened it in 2004. In 2014, Charlie and Nancy Frey purchased the Woods Inn and added a lakeside café platform and pavilion. Of the original fourteen Adirondack-style hotels on Fourth Lake, only the Woods Inn remains as a year-round business.

The grand hotel has experienced tragedy in its past and is incredibly haunted. Ed is one of the ghosts that haunts the building and grounds. Charles Edward "Ed" Duquette managed the hotel from 1903 until his death in an explosion in 1905. The hotel had installed a small power plant in order to illuminate the new electric lights. The power plant was located in a small shed behind the hotel. Unbeknownst to Ed, the power plant was poorly vented, and when the lights went out, he went into the small shed to evaluate the power loss. His lantern lit the accumulated fumes, blowing the shed and Ed to smithereens. Ed clung to life and spent his remaining days in agony, yet his soul returned to walk his beloved hotel. There were many sightings of Ed's ghost over the next one hundred years. During the time that the Woods Inn was owned and being renovated by Joedda McClain and Jay Latterman, a ghostly shadow figure was witnessed in the tavern. Ed continued to oversee the tavern and appeared during the remodeling. Many feel the iconic ectoplasm mist that was photographed as it swirled on the staircase was Ed. One employee was tapped on the shoulder, and one guest reported hearing a high-pitched noise in a closed room. The current owners have reported that they feel Ed's presence, and all agree that he is a friendly and curious ghost.

The Ghost Seekers of Central New York descended on the Woods Inn on a blustery, cold November evening to conduct a paranormal investigation that yielded everything from ghostly figures running down staircases, ectoplasm mists enveloping team members and voices to items being moved. The ghost of Ed was seen immediately by paranormal investigator David Peck as he was bringing the ghost hunting gear into the hotel. David was by the staircase that was captured in the famous ectoplasm photograph when he saw a white figure dart down the stairs and away. David followed and again saw the ghost dart around the corner. When David turned that corner, there was nobody there. Helen Clausen, Paranormal Ed Livingston and Dennis Webster started the investigation in room 206. While setting up the gear, lead investigator Bernadette Peck handpicked room 206 to investigate, as she smelled a foul, acrid odor emanating from the room. She went in, and her ghost senses were on full alert, so she sent the team there to interact with Ed and any other ghosts that might have been around.

The room was dark enough that you could not see your hands in front of your face; only the sliver of hallway light that came from the bottom of the door provided limited illumination. Right away, the team heard footsteps, movement and a growl and sensed more foul otherworldly odors that can only be described as pungent. Ed and Helen felt chills at the same time that Dennis felt something choking him. Dennis fled into the bathroom, leaving Ed and Helen alone in the creepy room 206. Dennis returned to the investigation, yet the interactions continued, with a strong smell of green apples and the sound of a chair sliding across the floor. While this was occurring, Bernadette and David witnessed a tablecloth in the dining room moving on its own, as if Ed was picking it up and pulling on it.

The Woods Inn is very haunted, and the ghostly interactions continued as the team moved its investigation to room 107, where the name Rose was picked up. When we tried to speak to her, we got a strong EVP that said, "Bullshit." The team heard footsteps in the hall and in the room that stopped and knocked. It was the intelligent haunting of a ghost. The climax in room 107 came when the ghost threw the Boo Bear talking ghost doll off the dresser and onto the floor. Then the entire room began to shake as if the spirits were agitated. The team fled the room but found no relief outside. Built next to the Woods Inn is a beautiful pavilion. It was out there where ghost seeker Helen felt the presence of Ed the ghost. When she asked for someone to take a picture, her entire body became enveloped in ectoplasm mist. She said it was friendly and warm, even though it was outside on a late November evening. This location was not far from where Charles Edward "Ed" Duquette died. There's no doubt that Ed's ghost lovingly walks the grounds and halls. I stopped by recently and met Brendan Simons, the caretaker. It was the offseason, and the hotel was empty. Brendan was kind enough to let me look at room 107, and as soon as I walked in, I became very ill and almost threw up. He told me that another ghost group had investigated the previous year and had found room 107 to be very haunted. I walked the outside perimeter and took some pictures of the grand structure. The next time you're in Inlet, be sure to stop by the Woods Inn, a haunted hotel on Fourth Lake that'll stun you with its beauty and raise your goosebumps with haunted rooms and spooky grounds.

Grace Brown's Ghost on Big Moose Lake
Eagle Bay

In the hot summer, down the road from Old Forge, a dastardly crime of murder in the early twentieth century left behind one of the most famous ghost stories in the United States. Big Moose Lake is the spot where, in July 1906, nineteen-year-old Grace Brown was tragically murdered at the hands of her lover, Chester Gillette. The murderer was executed in the electric chair for his crime, but it was Grace's ghost that would become the ghostly lady entity floating above the mountain lake waters. The crime created a national firestorm with a best-selling novel, *An American Tragedy*, and an award-winning movie, *A Place in the Sun*. Over one hundred years removed from the crime, there's still many who have witnessed the ghost of Grace Brown floating above the tragic waters.

Chester Gillette was a young man from wealth and privilege who was handsome and traveled the country before settling for a job in his uncle's skirt-making factory in Cortland, New York. The charming lad chased the skirts of all the young ladies, and the beautiful farmer's daughter Grace Brown caught his attention. Grace was born on March 20, 1886, on her family's farm in South Otselic, New York. She only grew to be five feet, two inches tall and weighed one hundred pounds, yet she was confident in the city, working as an inspector at the Gillette Skirt Factory. Chester charmed the shy girl, and Grace was head-over-heels in love. She became pregnant, and Chester showed his insidious love by booking a one-way murder trip to the Adirondack Mountains. Their journey would see the young couple stopping at the Hotel Utica before taking the train into the pine-covered mountains and ending at the Adirondack water of Big Moose Lake, where they stayed at the Glenmore Hotel. The locals thought it odd that the young couple had barely any luggage and that the young man was carrying a tennis racquet. Chester rented a boat and took Grace out for a nice row across the dark, still water. She was wearing a white button-up shirt and a light-green dress. Her brown hair was swept up, as was the fashion of the day. Chester brought his tennis racquet on the lake excursion, which he used to beat Grace on the head before dumping her body in the lake. Chester rowed ashore and fled, leaving behind his murdered girlfriend and unborn child. Chester ran until he ended up at the Arrowhead Hotel on Fourth Lake, where he got a haircut and spent the evening flirting with young ladies. The next morning, a search party sought out the missing couple, and Grace was

Left: The ghost of Grace Brown is seen hovering above Big Moose Lake. *Courtesy of the Town of Webb Historical Association.*

Right: Chester Gillette was put to death in the electric chair for the murder of Grace Brown. *Courtesy of the Town of Webb Historical Association.*

found, floating dead in a secluded bay of Big Moose Lake. Her lip was split, and she had an injury to her head. As they removed her body from the cold waters, blood ran from her nose. Wet locks of her hair had fallen across her pale and still face. Her spirit had already exited her body and begun its floating haunt above the dark waters, where it will stay for all eternity. Chester was later arrested for her murder. The tennis racquet was found in the woods next to the lake, hidden under a fallen pine.

It was the trial of the century at the Herkimer County Courthouse in Herkimer, New York. Chester's cell was covered with pictures and letters from throngs of young ladies who wanted to date the rich, handsome and charming murderer. Chester was found guilty of first-degree murder and was sentenced to die in the electric chair. The Casanova had shocked the nation by murdering the pregnant and innocent Grace Brown. To this day, it is one of the most tragic criminal cases in America. The handsome killer and dead pregnant lover captivated America, but it was the ghost of Grace that would be seen many times over the one hundred years since her death. Grace's ghost floating over the water of Big Moose Lake was featured on the television show *Unsolved Mysteries* and has been cited in many ghost books, both locally and nationally. Many visitors to the area have claimed to see her

Above: The Big Moose Lake Boathouse, where the fatal boat trip was launched. *Courtesy of the Town of Webb Historical Association.*

Opposite: Medium Josh Aust channels the spirit of Grace Brown from the spooky Big Moose Lake Gazebo. *Author's collection.*

apparition at night, drifting above the waters of Big Moose Lake. On the one hundredth anniversary of the murder, there was a wreath-laying ceremony. That night, Bernadette Peck from the Ghost Seekers of Central New York was there with friends, and they sat by the gazebo, when the waters were still and the moonbeams reflected across the black waters. It was then that Bernadette and her friends witnessed an apparition forming from the mist, and it developed into the form and entity of Grace Brown.

Bernadette returned in 2019 with her team members David Peck, Josh Aust and Dennis Webster. The Covewood Lodge is nestled next to Big Moose Lake and has the gazebo that was host to Bernadette's sighting of Grace's ghost. The group parked next to the closed Covewood, as it was not yet open for the summer season. The group walked around the beautiful lodge to get close to the water of Big Moose Lake when a couple of the caretakers came out and asked if we needed any help. Bernadette introduced herself

and the team, and the caretakers brought everyone into the front lobby of the Covewood. It was stunningly beautiful in its rustic charm. Bernadette and Josh felt the spirits right away. The caretakers described how they have encountered Grace's ghost many times in the lodge—so much so that when they are cleaning and working, she'll make noise, and they'll talk to her. They

The ghost of the murdered Grace Brown regularly stays at the Covewood Lodge, next to Big Moose Lake. *Author's collection.*

stated that the long green wooden footbridge on the water had been host to Grace's entity many times. People have seen her on the bridge, staring out over the calm inkwell water that took her life. The Covewood Lodge hosts people from all over the world who are moved by the tragic story of the murdered Grace Brown. The team was given permission to go over to the footbridge and gazebo. On the way over, the black flies were vicious and numerous in their swarming attack on us, yet when we got by the waters, they disappeared as if shooed away by an unseen presence. When the team got close to the footbridge, Dennis and Josh both had all the hairs on their arms stand up, and their bodies were buzzing. Bernadette was experiencing it as well, and the group recognized right away there was something there. Josh went and stood in the small gazebo and looked out over the dark waters, and he felt Grace's presence. Bernadette asked, "Grace, I was here long ago, and you appeared to me. Do you remember me?" She certainly did, as right after this, Josh closed his eyes to try to connect with Grace using his third eye or mental otherworldly abilities. Josh stated that Grace came to him and said she's at peace—she's calm. She told Josh that she loves the lake and that's why she chooses to stay there. When you visit, please be sure to talk to Grace's ghost. Over 110 years after her murder, and you can still witness Grace's spirit drifting across Big Moose Lake. She is the lady of the lake, whose tragic ghost, by paranormal choice, is forever shackled to the spot of her murder.

TOBOGGAN INN
EAGLE BAY

One the edge of Route 28 is a haunted pub where the ghosts love to throw silverware in the kitchen, move dishes from shelf to sink and stroke the hair of the owners and patrons. The Toboggan Inn is one seriously haunted building that's had a history of tragedy and fun on its nesting spot in Eagle Bay. The original building was constructed in the early twentieth century and had been used as an office space for the railroad that had tracks running not far behind the building. In the early 1930s, the building experienced a fire and lay vacant for many years, until Alfred Nelson rebuilt it and incorporated railroad ties into the back retaining wall and the floor as support beams. It was in the 1940s that the building was converted to a restaurant with apartments upstairs. It was then owned by Prentice and Al Wood, who named it the Toboggan Inn. Rumors of ghosts have been part of the Toboggan Inn ever since people started being in the building, all the time with voices and footsteps being heard. The restaurant was later sold and renamed the Hard Times Café. The building was sold to Mike and Vicky Beck in 2016, and they gave it the original name of the Toboggan Inn. But the Becks purchased the ghosts along with the building and furnishings. There was no extra charge for the ghosts—haunting came at no cost to their wallet, but it did come with a spiritual price. The Becks started remodeling

The spiritually overstuffed Toboggan Inn. *Author's collection.*

the building, and that's when the dormant or little-seen or -heard-of ghosts were activated with increased haunting events. It's a common occurrence to have spirits amplify their presence during the remodeling of a structure. It's as if they're cocooned within the walls and release on teardown. Another reason behind the increased haunting of the Toboggan Inn could be Mike and Vicky themselves, as they've experienced hauntings at other places they've lived; perhaps the spirits are attracted to the Becks and feel more comfortable appearing to them. In any case, the ghosts became more active once the Toboggan Inn roared back to life and welcomed hungry and thirsty patrons. Surely the ghosts were longing for what they could no longer have in the afterlife.

While Mike and his father, Dave, were remodeling, they heard footsteps when nobody else was in the building. Dave Beck was a nonbeliever and skeptic who now believes in hauntings and ghosts. Friends of the Becks who assisted with the remodel would also talk of working in the basement and hearing footsteps above or whispers and the voices of ladies talking in other rooms. When they'd go in these rooms, there was no one there, and the doors of the establishment were locked. There was so much activity

Toboggan Inn owners Mike and Vicky Beck talking to the ghosts with medium Josh Aust. *Author's collection.*

that Mike started cataloguing it in a logbook that he still keeps at the restaurant; it has many pages of paranormal activity. Many of the staff have experienced paranormal activity, including plates being thrown and Mike being scratched. Staff saw a chair in the dining room slide from a ghostly push. Vicky and Mike captured orbs on their security camera and a voice saying, "Stay quiet." Workers who were assisting Mike in the remodeling heard a female ghost say, "Shhhhh." As if their noise was bothering her. And they also heard ladies talking in another room, but when they walked in, they found there was nobody there. Dimes—yes, for some odd and yet unknown reason, the ghosts left ten-cent coins randomly around the Toboggan Inn, and now the Becks have a cup filled with them.

Mike and Vicky asked the Ghost Seekers of Central New York to come and investigate the building, and the night of the investigation proved that the Toboggan is, indeed, haunted and overstuffed with the supernatural. It was a quiet Saturday night in April, with the entire region on its seasonal shutdown. It was the time between winter sledding and summer sun and fun. The team included Bernadette Peck, David Peck, Mark Webster, Liz Bridgman, Joe Ostrander, Josh Aust and me. We were bringing in and setting up the ghost equipment when silverware was thrown in the kitchen. The paranormal fun was just beginning. I stayed and watched ghost central, where the night cameras were plugged in and showed the teams in action. Liz had said she saw the spirit of a little Black boy before the investigation began. She received the name Samuel. It didn't take long for the group on the second floor to interact with a grumpy male entity, while the group in the basement got the name of the little Black boy ghost, the same one Liz had seen. His name came through to me as Simon, and he said he liked to play the game Simon Says. The investigators felt Simon was afraid or held back from the male entity on the second floor. Two female entities roamed the dining room area and interacted with Mike, Vicky and Josh as the name Grace came through. Another name, ReRe, came through for the other female ghost (sometimes, ladies with the name Irene are called this). Mike was amazed, as his grandmother's name was Irene and his great-grandmother's name was Grace. During the investigation, Vicky had her hair stroked, and I had my neck stroked by Simon while I was in the basement with Josh and Dave. The Ghost Seekers of Central New York returned to go through the evidence with Mike and Vicky. They stated that, after the investigation, the security cameras picked up odd ectoplasm anomalies, doors opening and closing on their own and a toy piano playing upstairs on its own. The creepiest haunted event was when Mike's daughter was in the bar alone and heard a female voice say, "Stay quiet." There is no doubt that the ghost hunt proved the Toboggan Inn is a very haunted location. When you stop there for a drink and some food, you might just have your silverware thrown, your hair stroked or perhaps a dime left for you.

BRIGHTSIDE TRAINING CENTER
RAQUETTE LAKE

Once upon a time, there was a man who ran a corporation that purchased a beautiful hotel on an island in the middle of a lake of paradise in the Adirondacks that was converted into a world-class training center. The intelligent and curious came from far and wide to learn at the center, only to discover an education of the paranormal kind, as it was overstuffed with ghosts, entities and haunts. Fiber Instrument Sales (FIS), a company owned by businessman Frank Giotto, purchased the Brightside Hotel on an island in Raquette Lake in 2001 and spent a lot of time, money and love on updating

Brightside Hotel now hosts executive retreats that mesh with the ghosts of the haunted beauty. *Author's collection.*

the grand structure. It was turned into a beautiful training center that hosts the brightest and best from around the world to learn all about fiber optics. The Brightside was built in the latter half of the nineteenth century, when Joe and Mary Bryere were married and built the structure, around 1884. It was opened as a hotel in 1891 and received rave reviews on its grandeur and beauty from world travelers. *Paradise* was a word that was used quite

The haunted mother-in-law cabin at the Brightside Hotel. *Author's collection.*

often when describing the hotel. Joe operated the Brightside with fun and a love for all travelers until 1941. At the end of his tenure, he lost a leg due to frostbite and had to be carted around the property in a wheelbarrow. The Brightside operated on and off for many decades until it was sold to the industrious Frank Giotto, a successful businessman who also hosted retreats for many friends and family.

The Brightside has had haunted stories surrounding it for a long time, and they began when Billy Gestrich, one of the owners of the 1970s, told the tale of a young couple who was staying in the room above the kitchen. The husband went to cross the frozen lake in winter to run an errand, and his wife watched him disappear into a hazy blue fog. He disappeared, never to be seen or heard from again. She was overcome with sadness and would sit in the upstairs room, staring out the window at the water, waiting for her love to return. The wife died of a broken heart, yet her spirit has been seen looking out the window, waiting for her husband to come back to her. When the building was purchased in 2001 and remodeled, the construction workers found a lady's coat hanging in the closet of the haunted widow's room. The inspected it and found it was of the old style from the time the husband vanished and the widow's ghost appeared. They hung it back in the closet, and when they went back to the closet a few months later, there was a man's coat hanging next to the lady's that was of the same style and period. No one had come or gone from the room, so the theory is that the ghost of the husband had returned to his bride and hung his jacket next to hers. An interesting note on the Brightside is that Joe Bryere, the original owner, had served as the county coroner, and during the winter, when the ground was frozen solid, he would bring the bodies down into the basement and bury them in the soft dirt until the spring thaw, when they could be relocated and buried properly. The Brightside has had ghost hunters investigate and claims of paranormal activity abound. But the best personal experiences have been had by guests staying for training. One young lady retired early to her room, and when she was trying to read a book, the bed shook so violently that she fled downstairs, only to be reassured by the caretakers that she was in the ghost room and that the bed had done that for other guests—there was nothing to be afraid of. One gentleman woke up to blue orbs floating in his room. He checked out early.

I contacted John Bruno, the vice-president of training for the FIS Academy, and he obtained permission from the owner for me to tag along with a group of trainees and walk the Brightside. It was an honor and a privilege, as I know John had business to attend to yet accommodated me. It was a hot and sunny July day when I turned off Route 28 and crossed a bridge into Raquette Lake. I felt like I had crossed into another realm. The aura and zen in the air were unique and simple to me, and I sat by the water in front of the Raquette Lake Supply Company General Store, waiting for John and company to show up. It was long before the group arrived, and we boarded two pontoon boats that took us to the island. As we came around the bend and saw the Brightside, my entire body lit up with haunted anxiety, sort of like a paranormal gut punch. The structure was beautiful, but I could tell it was haunted even while I was still on the boat. The Brightside was majestic and brooding. Walking into the lodge, my breath was taken away by its beauty. John was kind enough to give me field notes from a ghost investigation. This team of paranormal investigators had witnessed a shadow person near the large stone fireplace, captured a ghost face looking out of the mother-in-law cabin out back and encountered a tall ghost figure up on the second floor. I was allowed to walk around freely as the guests were eating lunch and settling into their rooms. My ears were ringing, and when I went into the room on the second floor, where the widow went mad waiting for her lost husband to come back to her, I felt queasy, and my stomach was in knots. I talked to John briefly, and he said he had never experienced ghosts but had tried calling out to them. He's not skeptical but wants to see or experience something. I told him it would happen when he least expected it. Perhaps the ghosts of the Brightside like him, so they let him be.

I went into the basement, and it was beyond creepy, especially knowing that dead bodies used to be held in there. Who knows what spirits were left behind once the carbon, soulless human husks had been jettisoned to their permanent burial sites. It was thrilling and rather unsettling down there, so I quickly stepped back upstairs to chat with the caretakers. By this time, John had taken the trainees to another building to begin their professional fiber optic development. I sipped on a cold bottle of water and chatted with James Sudol and Henry Marshall, the caretakers of the Brightside. They also captain the boats to and from the mainland. James told me how, years ago, he used to stay in the mother-in-law cabin out back. One night in the middle of winter, when it was 0° Fahrenheit outside, he woke up sweating and had to get out of there. He said he was spooked, and his experience was confirmed by a ghost hunting team that said it was very haunted and that a demon possibly resided there. My paranormal curiosity was piqued, and I asked James if I could go sit in this haunted hot spot.

The cabin was warm and musty inside, as it no longer housed guests, but there was a small dresser with items on it and a small bed that had linens and pillows on it. This was around 2:00 p.m., so it was quite hot and sunny outside. This is usually not a prime ghost hunting time, but I thought I would try to connect. I took my shoes and eyeglasses off and lay on the bed. I closed my eyes and began to meditate. I practice Yoga Nidra, which is an ancient Hindu and Buddhist practice. What I was doing was getting into Sanskrit or "yogic sleep," in which you are in a state of meditated consciousness or "samadhi," in the realm of not awake but not asleep. It was in this realm that I connected to the ghost of the mother-in-law cabin. I could hear a glass mason jar that was on the dresser rattle and move. I stayed still. I dared not open my eyes, for I didn't want to view what was in there or hovering next to or above me. I had my rosary beads on me as my spiritual comforter and protection. I held them as I said in a calm gentle tone, "Give me a name." The ghost whispered in my ear, "Emily*." I said thank you, as it became sterile and quiet, and I knew the ghost had vanished. I got up and quietly put my eyeglasses and shoes back on. As I left the mother-in-law cabin, I bowed out of respect and appreciation.

When I walked into the Brightside, the look on my face was enough for James to ask what had happened. When I told him and Henry the story, their jaws dropped, and they told me Emily had been a regular guest at the Brightside and asked why a ghost would speak her name. I explained that I had asked the spirit to give me a name but didn't ask the ghost their name. It was quite obvious to me that this spirit was very fond of Emily and pleased to have her at the Brightside. Both understood, nodded and smiled at my explanation. I asked to be taken back to the mainland, as I had had enough of the island and the haunted Brightside. There was training going on, and my interference had to conclude. Henry was kind enough to break away from his duties and take me back to shore on his pontoon boat. On the ride, I commented on the beauty and the haunting feeling of the stunning Brightside. I gave appreciation for the honor of walking one of the most beautiful and haunted places in the Adirondack Mountains.

*The name has been changed.

ADIRONDACK HOTEL
LONG LAKE

On a breezy, wet, gray and chilly April day, I stopped by one of the most beautiful and historic hotels in the Adirondack Mountains. I pulled up just as snowflakes started to wisp by in sporadic numbers. I stopped outside and stared up at the hotel's grand beauty, and my mouth dropped. Surely the Adirondack Hotel has to have otherworldly guests. You must go and stay—just don't ask if it's haunted. Never in my ghost hunting or paranormal book writing career had I encountered a location where everyone, from the employees right up to the owners, said that their building did not have ghosts. I respect and honor their opinions; however, you might say I had my own paranormal event while staying at the Adirondack Hotel.

The jaw-droppingly beautiful Adirondack Hotel. *Author's collection.*

The hotel is breathtaking to look at, both inside and out, with its rustic, original charm and comfy rooms. The Adirondack Hotel is located on New York State Route 30, and its large verandas offer a breathtaking view of Long Lake. The hotel was built in the 1850s and is the only remaining hotel of its kind that is still operating in the Adirondacks. The original Kellog's Lake House burned to the ground in 1898 and was rebuilt in 1899. In 1914, a four-story addition was built that included eight more guest rooms and a formal dining room. The Adirondack Hotel was purchased in 1990 by Carol Young and has been completely restored to its former glory. Carol continues to upgrade and improve the hotel. And yes, she will tell you there are no ghosts in her hotel. It's not haunted.

I wanted to stay in the hotel, as I was heading up to Saranac Lake to spend the day with the Adirondack Park Paranormal Society (APPS). I stopped at the hotel at midday and loved the moose hanging on the wall behind the area where you check in. My room was on the second floor, and as I walked up and down the hall, my rosaries lit up. I'm Roman Catholic, so I'm spiritual and religious. I'm a member of the Ghost Seekers of Central New York; our team is spiritual and always prays before and after ghost hunts. I always wear my rosaries around my neck. They were hand made in New Mexico and blessed by a priest. I have worn them on dozens of paranormal investigations and never once had a reaction, but on the second floor of the Adirondack Hotel, they were burning my neck as they grew hot. I felt spiritual energy overwhelm me. I don't know who it was, but a ghost walked right through me while I was standing there. The feeling passed as quickly as it came, so I threw my overnight bag in my room on the second floor and then went for a walk.

I went up to the third floor, and there were housekeepers cleaning the rooms and changing the bed linens. I asked a young woman who had a bundle of linens in her arms if the Adirondack Hotel was haunted or if she had seen any ghosts. "No," she replied, rather curtly. "I believe in God." I walked away, shaking my head, as people will confuse ghosts with demons, darkness and evilness, but it's not that way if you talk to any of my teammates from the Ghost Seekers of Central New York. Ghosts can be friendly, curious and carry personalities to the afterlife. I asked about the top floor, and the employees told me it was locked down and nailed shut, as the fire codes of New York State would not allow a fourth floor in a wooden hotel. I was told the original woodwork is up there and that it's beautiful.

I left to go to Saranac Lake to walk through some haunted locations, but I returned in the early evening to go to the Adirondack Hotel Pub. I got the cheeseburger, fries and a cold beer. The staff was very friendly and the food delicious. It was open mic night, and the place was packed. It was so much fun, and I was having a great time, but I did get one ghost nugget on my way back to my room. I had an employee wave me to the side. They asked if I was the man who was writing and asking about ghosts. I nodded, and they told me that boaters who docked close to the shore on Long Lake had a view of the front of the hotel and the grand veranda. They said they had seen an entity looking out one of the fourth-floor windows. The employee said that no one goes up there, as it's locked and there's even insulation in the hallway and on floors. I nodded and respected the tale, but I could not verify the paranormal activity. But I did get something else from one of the guests.

I slept wonderfully in my room, without any disturbance, but I had hoped a ghost would come and greet me, especially after my rosaries had warmed up earlier in the day. There was a young couple who had stayed down the hall from me on the second floor, and when I introduced myself in the morning, they said their young son, who was eight years old, had seen something that scared him walking down the hall, and then it was gone. In many instances, children can see the unseen—they can see things that us adults cannot. I did not doubt the experience of this boy, as it happened in the exact location of my goosebumps and rosary bead heat-up. But I do have to respect the opinion of the owners and the staff of the Adirondack Hotel, who declare in a firm manner the hotel is not haunted. I would say never say never in our mortal realm, as those who have the gift of a third eye can sometimes pierce the veil of the other side and see that which others declare invisible. And I would highly recommend you stay at the beautiful and engaging Adirondack Hotel—even just for comfort, commensuration, burgers and brews.

P-2's Irish Pub
Tupper Lake

Searching for ghosts is a pursuit of the soul. When I was in Tupper Lake, researching haunted locations, I came across a loving haunted place without even looking for it. Fate and spirits collided when I was driving through downtown Tupper Lake, looking for a place to get a cold beer after a day of chasing the paranormal. I had every intention of hitting up a business on the other side of town that had been recommended to me by a town resident in the parking lot of the village gas station. But as I was driving, I saw a brick building with a sign that said, "P-2's Irish Pub." I did a double take, as there was something that drew my attention. I made a U-turn in my pickup truck and parked next to the pub. I got out and could hear music coming from the other side of the building; I was thrilled to have entertainment. As soon as I walked inside, I felt a cool, paranormal vibe. The interior had charming décor and was packed with local residents, eating, drinking and laughing—in good spirits.

I ordered Raquette River Mango, a local microbrew that was frosty, foamy, cold heaven in a chilled glass. I went out in the adjacent yard, sat alone at a table and watched a very entertaining musical act called Mingo & Big Boss Sausage. There was a nice crowd bopping to the tunes. I was sipping my beer, all alone, as is my usual author ghost mode, when a lady sat down and greeted me. Her smile was bright, and her eyes sparkled as she asked, "Who are you? I know everybody, but I don't know you." I said I was a writer researching haunted places and that there was something about this place that drew me in. She introduced herself as the owner, Michelle LeBlanc Blair, and said that it was interesting I had stopped there, as her father's spirit was in the bar, his most beloved place. I was intrigued. Her father's birth name was Joseph Alexander LeBlanc, but he was born small and petite, so he was given the name P-2 as a nickname, and the moniker stuck for the rest of his life. The building has been around since the 1920s, but from 1946 to 1966, it was called Ivan's Lounge. P-2 worked there and

P-2's Irish Pub hosts the owner's spirit and friendly locals of Tupper Lake. *Author's collection.*

loved the place so much that he purchased it and renamed it "Al's Lounge Meet You at P-2." The name would eventually be changed to P-2's Irish Pub. P-2 was placed in an assisted living facility in 2006 but would always be seen at his favorite spot in the pub, smoking and entertaining family and friends.

Michelle told me that P-2's spirit is in the pub, as she and all the staff feel his presence. P-2 is always with her, and she feels him in her car while she's driving and, one time, when she was out on the lake under a clear blue sky. She explained that her father would always flirt with the ladies in the pub and that he would make the "OK" sign and look through, so he was known for this gesture.

Joseph Alexander "P-2" LeBlanc. *Courtesy of Michelle LeBlanc- Blair.*

So, she was out on the boat, talking to her father, when, out of nowhere, a cloud with a perfect circle formed. Michelle knew this was her father telling her everything was going to be OK. I left that night feeling the love of P-2's and knew why it was so revered and why he would stick around.

I was back in town a few months later and decided to stop in on a cold, rainy Saturday night to have a burger and a beer. I walked in, and Michelle was there to greet me with smile and warm hug. I went and sat in her father's favorite spot. She pointed out with affection the burn marks on the bar from her father's cigarettes. I was thrilled Mingo was going to be performing. A very talented man was behind the microphone, and I'm sure P-2 was going to be there to enjoy every moment. I was given an ice-cold draft by Emily Martin, the talented photographer and bartender, and I struck up a discussion about P-2. She told me that the light above the bar flickers and that everyone is convinced that it's him, as it'll flicker especially when politics is the topic of discussion. Michelle had told me the same story before and that many electricians had looked the light and the wiring, yet it would still flicker. Emily cracked me up by saying the raccoon was her spirit animal because she stays up late, eats trash and has dark circles under her eyes. She explained she's a skeptical observer and will believe it when she sees it. I explained that's acceptable, as most people will experience a ghost for the first time when a loved one dies and pays a paranormal visit before transcending to another plane.

Sitting in P-2's favorite spot, I could see why he chose it, as you can see everyone coming and going from the pub; the kitchen door is directly behind you, so you can smell the food cooking; and him being a big flirt, it makes sense that the ladies' room is to your right. All the ladies visit the porcelain palace once the beverages flow down their giggling gullets. I spoke to the other bartender, Cassandra Lamboy, and she feels P-2's presence and knows he is there. She said she was once brushed on the shoulder by an entity. Mingo was playing an entertaining version of the song "Cover of a Rolling Stone" when I went over and sat next to Michelle to discuss her father and the pub. She gave me a copy of a photograph of P-2 and beamed as I looked at it, complimenting his smile.

There's no doubt that ghosts love. They maintain their personalities and emotions into the afterlife, and I felt P-2's presence, especially when I sat in his beloved spot at the bar, drank a beer, ate a burger and watched the local ladies dance to the music of Mingo. So, the next time you're going through Tupper Lake, be sure to stop at P-2's Irish Pub, where the spirit of a loving person might flicker a light for you.

The Oval Wood Dish (OWD) Company
Tupper Lake

Driving down the main drag of the town of Tupper Lake, one cannot help but notice the tallest structure that looms over the entire town and lake like a brick overlord across the street from Raquette Pond: the smokestack of the Oval Wood Dish Company, with the large initials "OWD" painted on it. Right next to the smokestack is a water tower that's almost equal in height but has a greater girth. The pair look like twin aliens right out of *War of the Worlds*. I drove past them on my way to another haunted location down the road, so I pulled into the parking lot and just stared at these iconic beacons, along with the massive adjacent factory. It's one of those places that looks haunted, but I wasn't sure, as I knew nothing about the place. Little did I know that my bloodhound-like paranormal nose would lead me to a place that's a host to ghosts. I got in my truck and left, looking in my rearview mirror at the twin overlords as I went along my way. I would be back.

The Oval Wood Dish (OWD) Company started construction of the factory in 1916 and cut its first log in 1918; it made wooden spoons, forks and bowls. It quickly became an economic force in the Adirondacks, and at one time, it employed 10 percent of the population in Tupper Lake. Sales declined, and the company was sold in 2003 to the Jarden Corporation, but

The decayed OWD Plant in Tupper Lake hosts ghostly workers. *Author's collection.*

it only lasted until 2008, when it closed its doors. A sad decline for OWD, which had, at one time, owned 100,000 acres in the Adirondacks. It now houses a storage business and perhaps spirits.

I got back to the Tupper Lake Hotel, where I was spending the night, and walked up to Tyler Schuller, the son of the owner, Heidi Schuller. He was out in front of the hotel office, sitting on a bench, sanding the doors from the hotel's kitchen cabinets. I struck up a conversation and gave him one of my business cards that says "paranormal investigator" on them. "You a ghost hunter?" he asked, and I nodded. I asked Tyler if the OWD was haunted, as it lured me off the main road with its humongous, ominous presence. He stopped working, stood up and told me that he was with a buddy once—it was midnight and as dark as the night would ever be—when they decided to check out the factory. They parked their truck and were walking out back when they felt something around them. When they were getting into their truck, Tyler said a ghost ran right in front of them, and his friend was frightened. They ran straight out of there.

It was at this time that Heidi Schuller came out to talk to me and said she worked in OWD when it was making plastics for the Jarden Corporation. She was working the night shift in the plant and said that everyone would state how scary it was at night and that they all heard things. Heidi told me that, one night, she was in an area all alone when all the hair on the back of her neck stood up. She started to feel sick to her stomach, so she stopped working and fled the plant, only to feel fine once she left the building and crossed the property's threshold. She said it was not the plastics that made her ill but the spirits.

I was intrigued, so I decided to go back down to OWD at midnight. I drove down and put my truck in the grocery store parking lot next door. I got out and leaned against the bed of my pickup truck, just looking at the smokestack and water tower guardians. It was quiet, except for a few crickets chirping in the crisp summer moonlight. I had not received permission to go into the building, so I decided to just walk around the back and see if I could feel or see anything. I was compelled to go there, but I caution the reader against replicating my odyssey, as one must have the blessing of an owner. I took the risk, figuring I'd spend the night in the town jail, have my shinbone gnawed on by a junkyard dog or get generously sprayed by a waddling skunk. Once I got behind the large main OWD building, a large cloud crossed in front of the moon, and I was thrown into complete darkness. Like a fool, I had left the flashlight in the cab of my truck. My heart raced as I fumbled with my cellphone, trying to get it to illuminate, but I had no luck. I froze as I felt the hair on my arms raise up. Suddenly, the crickets went silent. I listened intently, as there was no junkyard dog. There was nothing there but the drum of my racing heart in my creeped-out body.

It was then that I could hardly believe what I was hearing. I could hear chains rattling inside the building—a ghost rattling them at me. Never had I heard paranormal iron links shaking at me in all my years and many investigations. I could hardly breathe as I tiptoed out of there, leaving behind the entity of a lost soul. I hadn't expected to encounter this, and once I was safe inside the cab of my truck, I shook my head in disbelief and wished the chain-rattling ghost had told me their name. I can only imagine the haunted experiences that'll await any ghost-hunting team that is ever granted permission to explore the goliath landmark. I drove away holding my rosary beads and whispering a prayer under my breath.

HOTEL SARANAC
SARANAC LAKE

The weather was dreary and cold. It was midday, the sky was gunmetal gray and the clouds blocked the spring sunrays. It was April in the Adirondacks, and I was going to see the Adirondack Park Paranormal Society (APPS), as they were going to bring me to see the Hotel Saranac and give me all the details of it and their ghost investigation. This was the first time I met APPS leader Damon Jacobs and his crack paranormal squad. They had been highly recommended to me when I contacted some Lake Placid historians. I was pleased that Damon and company would meet with me and give me a personal tour of Hotel Saranac.

I had heard of Hotel Saranac, as its haunting is legendary and well known among ghost enthusiasts. This grand dame of architectural design sits smack-dab in the center of the village of Saranac Lake. My jaw dropped on the tour, as the place is astoundingly beautiful. The Hotel Saranac is known for its second-floor great hall that is designed in and influenced by the fourteenth-century Palazzo Davanzati style from Florence, Italy, with ornate paintings and breathtaking décor. The Hotel Saranac opened on July 1, 1927, and was an instant hit with modern amenities, including one hundred baths. The 1932 Winter Olympics were held down the road in Lake Placid in 1932, and Hotel Saranac was sold out for five months straight.

The APPS crew was able to investigate in April 2014, when the hotel was in the midst of a large remodel that took four years and cost $35 million. Paranormal investigators will tell you that remodeling tends to stir up the spirits or amplify their activities. The APPS investigators spent two entire nights in the hotel, conducting spiritual research. The team included Damon Jacobs, Susan Goff, Mat Morgan, Penny Colburn, Melissa Conto, Kaylynn Conto, Karen Page, McKayla Gunderson, Alyssa Farrell and Ann Farrell. The APPS team brought all of their scientific ghost hunting equipment, including digital recorders, electromagnetic handheld devices and night vision video cameras. These devices are used to record and verify, but the highly skilled team of investigators had their minds, hearts and souls set on receiving communication from those who are no longer among the breathing.

Hotel Saranac is a large structure with many floors and rooms, but the APPS team had the advantage of Susan Goff, a crack researcher and a former employee of the hotel. Susan discovered that the property had

Hotel Saranac hosts guests of the ghostly variety. *Author's collection.*

formerly been the site of the Saranac High School and that the structure burned to the ground. The hotel was built on the leftover foundation of the school. There's the male ghost that's been seen in the basement, adorned in a top hat and tails. People theorize it's the spirit of Howard Victor "Prof" Littell, a beloved Saranac High School administrator from the early twentieth century. The other famous ghost is that of Emily Balsam, who lived in the hotel and passed away in room 310 at the age of seventy-three on January 11, 1983. Emily was found peacefully deceased on her bed, with her cat asleep on her chest. Susan had experienced paranormal events when she was an employee of the Hotel Saranac, including hearing the cries of a ghost cat, hearing a phantom cat scratching on the walls and seeing imprints on beds in the shape of an unseen cat. Former employees were interviewed by Damon and the APPS team, and they told tales of water faucets turning on, singing and humming, doors slamming, doorknobs rattling and one housekeeper who had been pushed from behind by a spirit. There's no doubt the Adirondack Park Paranormal Society was stepping into a hotbed of otherworldly activity.

APPS granted me unprecedented access to its files from the investigation. The report is very detailed and is overstuffed with spiritual activity and verification of the legends. It was a mix of their art and science that proved the case. Mat Morgan is the team's spiritual nerve center, as he's a medium, shaman and medicine man whose third eye assists the team on their spiritual safari. During the investigation, Mat picked up on spiritual energy in room 613. During this time, the temperature dropped, and he smelled cigar smoke. Mat intervened when one of the investigators was pinned to a wall and paralyzed in place. Mat referred to this entity as Tim. His intervention sent the ghost on its way, and the unharmed investigator went back to their normal humanistic state. Sue heard her name called and saw a shadow person peering from behind a pillar in proximity to the kitchen entrance. The freakiest and wildest paranormal event occurred when a tripod that was holding a video camera fell over. There were no human beings on the floor of the hotel, and absolutely no one was near the tripod. It takes a massive amount of otherworldly spiritual strength to manifest, let alone knock a fully laden tripod to the ground.

APPS was granted a second investigation during the spring of 2020 and brought along a special guest investigator, Dennis Webster from the Fort Schuyler Paranormal Society (FSPS). The APPS team included lead investigator Damon Jacobs, Sue Murphy-Goff, Matheau Morgan, Marcy Brunet, Amy Lynn Fisk, Jessica Trombley, Destiny Allen, Paul Allen and Jennifer Coriale. The team encountered footsteps under a bed and voices from the other side; the largest paranormal event occurred in the basement. The team had an antique black top hat and placed it on the shelf next to the bottom of the stairs. There was a camera pointed at the hat. And during the evening, when there were no investigators in the basement, the hat moved.

APPS provided me with its investigative notes on their observations and experiences, and there were certainly more than enough ghosts for the hotel to earn the honor of being one of the top-ten most haunted hotels in the United States. The APPS team used new technical equipment, like digital video cameras and gauss meters, but they also used old-school ghost items, like dowsing rods and a pendulum. Marcy had the name "Jim" come to her the night before the investigation, and this was the entity the team encountered on the second floor, in the hallway. Room 613 was active, with the ghosts answering through the pendulum that they didn't like one of the investigators in the room. This investigator, Brett, suddenly had difficulty breathing, had something slap the temperature gauge he was holding out of his hand and forced him to flee the room.

Animals can also be ghosts, with their spirits wandering the realm of human ghosts, and the APPS team had a first-person interaction when investigator Aymee-Lynne felt a ghost cat rub up against her leg when she was in room 620. The APPS had many spiritual interactions, and they were strong, certifying Hotel Saranac as haunted and paranormal. The ghosts are active and bountiful within Hotel Saranac. "In our professional paranormal experience, the Hotel Saranac contains spiritual energy. But, no fear, as we feel the ghosts haunting the hotel are not harmful or dangerous. Staff and guests are safe," said Damon Jacobs. Stay the night, and perhaps you'll be greeted by "Prof" in his ghostly top hat and tails.

PALACE THEATRE
LAKE PLACID

Beware of ghosts who go bump in the night, especially when you're in a movie theater, watching a movie and munching on hot buttered popcorn. The historic and grand Palace Theatre hosts ghosts in its majestic theatrical bosom. Little did I expect that walking the rows of seats would lead to a paranormal event of the intelligent haunted variety and, within seconds, verify the Palace Theatre as a showplace for a mystical, otherworldly creature. The Palace Theatre was built on Main Street in Lake Placid and opened to a joyful Adirondack public on May 29, 1926, a downtown icon, along with the region's winter activities and the Olympics that were held there in 1932 and 1980. The theater was purchased in 1961 by Reg Clark and has been in the family ever since. The Palace Theatre has undergone the conversion

Left: The Palace Theatre in downtown Lake Placid. *Author's collection.*

Below: Ghosts wander the seats of the Palace Theatre. *Author's collection.*

from 35-mm movies to digital, but its beautiful originality still exists, making it quite the gem. It's no wonder the ghosts stick around.

I was in Lake Placid right in the middle of its Ironman event. The village and surrounding area were overrun with world-class athletes, primping, preening, running and biking over every available nook and cranny. I shoved peanut butter crackers in my mouth as I admired their athletic dedication. I was going to be flexing my paranormal muscles, which demands highly salted snacks. I parked my truck and strolled downtown, as it was the middle of July, and the sun was blazing extra hot that day. I walked into the Palace Theatre and had to blink my eyes for a few minutes to get my rods and cones to adjust to the dark interior. My nostrils flared with delight at the smell of fresh artificially buttered movie theater popcorn. There was a lady behind the counter, filling paper bags with the popcorn, and she said hello with a bright smile. There was no one in the theater, so I looked at the marquee; it showed that the next movie wasn't to start for another hour.

The woman behind the counter introduced herself as Kim Clark, the owner's daughter. I introduced myself as a paranormal investigator and an author who was looking to write about the Palace Theatre. I had read it was haunted and was thrilled I was speaking to a person who would know firsthand. Kim said the theater was haunted and that they had some photographs from the inside that had ghosts in them. I asked her if it would be OK for me to walk around the theater. I got a big yes, so I quietly wandered the larger lower theater. I sat in one of the seats and marveled at the beauty. The originality was a wonder to behold. I sat for a few minutes, jotting in my journal, taking in every detail in regard to the décor. It felt kind of flat, so I decided to get up and wander, which is my nature as a ghost seeker and human with that curious id that can be a blessing.

I went back to the lobby, and Kim was nowhere to be seen, so I looked, and to the right and left of the lobby were stairs. Something compelled me to take the stairs to the right, the ones near the men's room. I walked up and was pleased to discover a very small theater, with no more than fifty seats. I wandered and sat where my body felt compelled. I started to write in my journal. Suddenly, I felt woozy and lightheaded; I had shortness of breath and got a feeling of very good juju. It was a good vibe. My ears started ringing, and then I heard footsteps. They were coming behind me, and I froze for a second, as I knew I was the only mortal in the room. It was empty when I had strolled in there, and no one had followed me. I put my pen in my journal, closed it and looked to the back-right corner. I was astounded to see a full-body entity of a man staring at me. He jutted to the right in a quick fashion and went through the wall. For a second, I didn't think I had seen what I really saw. I was astounded and never expected to encounter a ghost—at least not in that type of seeking. Many ghost hunters will tell you that you'll see a spirit when you least expect it, and this was the case for me.

I got up slowly and walked to the spot of his appearance; I felt the spot on the wall where his entity had gone through, and it felt cold. I pulled my hand back and wiped it on my shirt. All of the sudden, I had a shortness of breath and decided to go back downstairs. Kim was back behind the counter and stopped filling the popcorn bags when I walked up. I had a blank look and set my journal on the glass-top counter that had all the candies and gummies displayed below. I told Kim what I had seen, and she smiled and said, "You saw George." Others have seen his ghost up there. Others have seen a little girl ghost in here as well. I can guarantee you, based on my experience as a ghost seeker and paranormal investigator, that the Palace Theatre is 100 percent certified haunted. Perhaps the next time you're in there, watching a movie, George might come and sit right next to you. Be sure to tell him to buy his own popcorn.

STAGECOACH INN
LAKE PLACID

Sometimes, in life, you walk into a building, and it's love at first sight. What's not to adore about the Stagecoach Inn—the over-150-year-old rustic charm, the breathtaking view of the mountains and the ghosts that haunt the antique-laden rooms. The Stagecoach Inn has a long and rich history. The area was known for Osgood's Inn, as the Osgood family had been prominent, but it was not located in the same building as the Stagecoach, although it was close by. Sue Goff and Jessica Trombley conducted a vast amount of research for the Adirondack Park Paranormal Society (APPS) in order to have a good ghost investigation. They were kind enough to share their findings with me.

The inn's original name was the Lyon's Inn, named after the original owners, Martin and Amanda Lyon, and it was opened in 1864. The inn had many rooms, each with a fireplace, and it hosted a general store and a post office. It was a popular destination for locals and tourists. The Lyon's Inn was also a stop on the stagecoach route that was run before the railroad came through in 1893. Lyon's Inn went out of business in 1900. It became a private residence for many years and was even owned by Melvil Dewey, the

The historic and iconic Stagecoach Inn. *Courtesy of the Adirondack Park Paranormal Society (APPS).*

creator of the Dewey Decimal System and the founder of the Lake Placid Club. Peter Moreau and his wife purchased the property in 1977 and spent a lot of time and money restoring the place, renamed the Stagecoach Inn, to its former glory. An attic fire in 2002 devastated part of the building, but it was restored by the current owners. The current owners, Michael and Stacia Takach, were kind enough to agree to have their establishment ghost hunted and investigated for paranormal activity.

I worked with the APPS on a two-night investigation and ghost hunt to see if we could verify the stories of the spooky. It was mid-November, and the temperature hovered around 0° Fahrenheit—even the snow was shivering. I arrived a few hours before APPS was due to be there and met the innkeeper, Laina Hamilton, whose sweet charm bubbled from her southern roots. She was a Dixie transplant in the wonderful frozen North. She showed me to my room, the "Osgood Suite." The Stagecoach was going to be closed down for the weekend, and Laina would be staying in her room on the backside of the inn, so I was pretty much alone in the structure—a writer locked in a haunted inn during the midst of winter. It was like something out of a movie. I knew nothing of the haunted happenings or what APPS had discovered in its historical research or walkthrough. I wanted to come in with a clear mind.

I was putting my things away in my suite when I saw a coat hanger with a lantern attached hanging on the rod in the closet. I slid it to the right and proceeded to hang my jacket on it and put my travel bag on the floor below. I went and sat on the bed and was writing in my journal when I heard a loud bang. I went and looked, and the coat hanger and

The Stagecoach Inn hosted many Adirondack travelers. *Courtesy of the Stagecoach Inn.*

lantern were on the floor. I inspected it, and it had to have been lifted and thrown by a ghost. The APPS team looked it over when they arrived and couldn't debunk it. I had a ghost in my room that didn't like his stuff touched or moved—fascinating. Laina was kind enough to give me a walkthrough and told me previous ghost experiences that had happened to guests. There was a couple who had recently stayed in the Martin Lyon Room on the second floor, and in the middle of the night, the door started rattling, and the doorknob began turning. They jumped out of bed and opened the door to nothing but air. Nikki, the housekeeper at the Stagecoach Inn, had been doing her work when the television in the lounge came on with the Home and Garden Channel blasting. She was startled, as there was no one there.

The ghosts of the inn sure like watching television, as the owner, Stacia, had her own paranormal experience in the Dewey Day Room on the second floor. She was leaving the room and shut off the television. She got all the way down the stairs when she heard a noise. She walked back up into the Dewey Day Room and the television was on. She shrugged her shoulders and shut it off. She walked down and, again, it came on. She walked into the room and spoke the phrase she's famous for, "Holy heck, cut it out."

She shut the television off, walked all the way down the stairs and—you guessed it—it came on again. She walked into the room, shut the television off and said to the playful ghost, "Please don't do this to me." That time, the television stayed off, and Stacia had her husband, Michael, come to look at the appliance. He found nothing that would cause the television to come on all by itself. Stacia said she loves the fact that her beautiful establishment has ghosts; she just doesn't want to see one.

Laina captured a spirit in a photograph she took inside the owner's quarters. She had a bouquet of pink roses on the dresser and took a few pictures. When she looked at them later, one of the photographs captured the ghost of a lady wearing a hat in the mirror. The spirit was admiring the flowers. Laina had another experience with candles coming out of their candlesticks. She kept putting the candles in the candlesticks and setting them on the large main fireplace mantel, but when she came back, they appeared as if they'd been removed with force. On my walkthrough, I was on the second floor of the Dewey Day Room when I got chills and halted. I told Laina that the spot freaked me out and that I didn't know why. I would find out why very soon.

There was no doubt that the APPS team was excited to investigate the Stagecoach Inn to see if any of these experiences could be validated. The team, for the first night, included team lead and founder Damon Jacobs; Sue Goff, case manager; Ann Farrell, team lead; Jessica Trombley, investigator; Jim Bankic, medic; Aymee-Lynne "Alf" Fisk, investigator; and Destiny-Faith Roberts, secretary. I was asked to come along as a consultant and was thrilled to be working with APPS. Sue arrived first and asked me if I felt anything on the walkthrough. When I told her about the spot I got freaked out in, she smiled and said Damon had the same "off" feeling from the spot. Then Sue said that she had a dream that I was lying on the bed in that room, meditating, with an entity circling around me, bending over and inspecting me with otherworld curiosity. There's no doubt our third eye gifts were aligning. This was a good sign for the ghost hunt.

The first night was fully stuffed with paranormal investigative talent, as the APPS team included Damon, Sue, Ann, Jessica, Alf, Jim and Destiny. The command center, which is the nerve center of any paranormal investigation, was located in the front foyer, where guests check in. While the APPS team was running cameras and stringing wires to power them, there was ghostly activity kicking in. Ann was standing in the doorway to the command center when she heard a lady singing a gentle "hmmm, hmmm, hmmm." Jim was in the closet where the lantern and hanger were thrown. He was trying to

Left: A rosary of the author that was broken by a ghost. *Author's collection.*

Opposite: The haunted Irish Bar at the Stagecoach Inn. *Author's collection.*

debunk the incident and wasn't having any success when he got a very cold chill on the back of his neck. Alf was setting up a camera in the dining room when a large wooden door opened up and smacked into her. The APPS team tried to debunk this incident and could not replicate it. Sue and Ann were talking in the large sitting room with the main fireplace when they saw a shadow figure in the window that had the stagecoach etched into it.

Laina, the innkeeper, left and locked herself in her room in the back of the upstairs area of the inn. She had a book, and we didn't hear a peep from her until the end of the night. The gear was all set up, and the spiritual safari was set in motion. The first team to deploy included Sue, Ann and me, and we headed up to the second-floor room where Damon, Sue and I had sensed a paranormal lure. I decided to lie down on the bed up there and just breathe and relax while Sue and Ann started to communicate with the other side. I suddenly felt a heavy weight on my chest and said, "I think something just sat on my chest." Ann said, "I see it. It's a child sitting on your chest." I was not freaking out, as it was a curious ghost. When the child left, the pressure was gone, and I said nothing when Ann said, "I saw her leave, she's gone." It was right after this that Sue saw an entity standing behind the camera.

This was the theme of both nights; the entity was too shy to approach and would stand back. The night continued to be active, as Ann was poked in the back and Destiny got a strong cigar scent that she said smelled like a Swisher Sweet. Paranormal activity can produce smells. Jess and Alf were crossing the threshold to the second floor when the mel meter went from 0.0 to 8.1, a huge spike. This could have indicated the presence of a ghost, as it was not able to be debunked. Electrical devices and wires can cause spikes, but there was nothing of that sort in the spot. Damon, Jim and Jess tried the second floor, with Damon deploying his dowsing rods. These are old-school ghost hunting tools, but they quite effective. At first, Damon was getting wonderful interaction when, all of a sudden, everything went flat.

The teams regrouped to conduct an EVP session on the first floor, where the Irish bar is located. Damon saw a shadow entity standing back in the corner and tried to coax it to come closer. He asked if it was from the Underground Railroad. Abolitionist John Brown had his Lake Placid farm just down the road, so it made sense that the spirit could have been that of a runaway slave. The entity would not approach and disappeared. The first night wrapped up with a good night of ghost interaction. Everyone left, and I went in my room. I was settling in for sleep when I heard a loud boom, as if someone had stomped their foot on the wood floor outside my room. I went and opened my door, but there was no one there. "Welcome to the haunted Stagecoach Inn," I said as I smiled, shut my door and slumbered.

The second night of ghost hunting was conducted with a much smaller group: Sue, Ann and me. We asked Laina to be with us as a trigger object, since the spirits liked her energy. I must be the southern charm she brings to the frozen North. We went with just handheld devices and a single handheld video camera. The Stagecoach Inn was pitch black with all the lights off, and it was as quiet as a church mouse. We started out in the small sitting room on the first floor, and Laina asked if anyone was there when Sue saw a little girl ghost peeking around the corner at the top of the stairs. Names were suggested—like Jenny—but the little girl ghost responded to Mary. We found out that Mary Osgood had lived in that area and passed away at the age of six in the mid-nineteenth century. Then we all saw the ghost of a man in the other room, standing behind a birch pole. I saw him moving, and my heart leapt into my throat. Seeing ghosts never ceases to spike the adrenaline. The ladies asked if it was Hiram Lusk, who the group felt was the man in the painting who looked like the man in Sue's dreams. We then moved up to the second floor, and this male entity followed us. I had a feeling he did not like my rosaries. I always wear them on paranormal investigations, and Ann and Sue felt it was the spirit of a preacher, deacon or Protestant who felt none too kindly about a Catholic flaunting their crucifix. Sue always has hers as well, but she keeps hers hidden. Meanwhile, mine hangs on my chest outside of my shirt.

The scariest interaction from both nights occurred when the group went into the room where the pink roses had produced a female ghost in the mirror. We purchased roses to bring the female ghost forth, but it was the male ghost who followed us. Laina and Ann sat on the bed while Sue and I stood back. It was so dark you could barely see a few feet in front of you. We were talking to the spirits when Laina and Ann said the blankets on the bed were rippling. A ghost was coming up the covers, toward them. I leaned in to see, so my rosaries were hanging off my chest. Suddenly, Ann shrieked. I jumped back and swore a blue streak from fright. Ann, normally super cool under paranormal fire, said she had closed her eyes for a few seconds, and when she opened them, there was a male ghost looking at her. His face was inches from hers. It took me a few seconds before I realized my rosaries were missing. I turned the flashlight on, and there they were on the floor, broken. They had not gotten snagged on anything; the male entity must've held them, and when I jerked back, they snapped. There was no other explanation. I had the feeling this spirit was a Methodist preacher. I have no evidence of this, but I had been a Methodist throughout my youth before converting to Catholicism. Today, I'm spiritual and not a practitioner of any strand of religion. I just feel I like I know Methodists, and his reaction to my Catholic necklace was appropriate for that belief.

We went back into the kitchen to take a break, and I fixed my rosary with pliers before putting them back on. Our last round saw us go into the first -floor bedroom that had been the master suite, as it had the largest fireplace of any of the rooms. This was the Genny Room, and this was the first time the ghosts started to touch the handheld ghost detection devices, causing them to blat and blare sounds and colors. This interaction was the result of Ann, Laina and Sue asking if the little girl Mary was with us and if the dog in the painting was hers. In the main livingroom, there is a painting of a brown dog with a white blaze on its chest. The response was greatest when Laina and Sue were asking the name of the puppy. "Marty, Molly," then the largest response—"Magnolia." We ended the evening exhausted but smiling.

Everyone left, and Laina went to her room upstairs, so I was all alone in the downstairs area. I went to my room and locked the door from the inside. That would stop only solid humanity, as ghosts could just walk through. The spirits can be rude, and perhaps personal space violations are not a rule of the afterlife. I took off my rosary and placed it on the dresser. I decided to put the rem pod and my ghost meter in my room. These devices illuminate when a ghost is nearby. I turned off all the lights, crawled into my squishy comfy bed and tried to fall asleep when the devices began buzzing and flashing red, yellow and green lights that lit up the dark night. I was too tired to be scared, so I got up, shut off the devices, lay back down, pulled the covers up to my chin and joined the sandman. I awoke when I felt the sunbeams cracking through the blinds, warming my face. I yawned, sat up and looked in shock and disbelief at my rosary, as it had been thrown to the floor and ripped apart. It was obvious that the Methodist preacher ghost really didn't like my rosary. I was not angry but apologized to the spirit if I offended him, as I meant no harm. Sue had a great theory that, along with the preacher and little girl entity, one entity was that of a former innkeeper. So, it made sense that this entity would not like interlopers sitting on the beds, placing their hats on the beds or wearing shoes in the house. Damon and Sue both felt the ghosts were intelligent in the Stagecoach Inn, which means they can interact with you. There's no doubt that the Stagecoach Inn was certified 100 percent haunted by the APPS team. All of the rooms have ghosts, so when you stay, take your pick, and who knows what spirit might greet you in your nightly slumber.

PULPIT ROCK
LAKE PLACID

The body of the "Lady of the Lake" had sat in the dark frigid depths for thirty years before it was discovered and dragged out into the Adirondack air, exposing the perfectly preserved body. Yet the ice-cold waxy husk had left behind the spirit that had escaped from the drowned woman, and it now haunts Pulpit Rock of Lake Placid for all eternity. The woman's name was Mabel Smith Douglass, and her ghost has been seen by many tourists, townspeople and the curious for over eighty-five years. Her spirit has been seen hovering above the waters and peering up from the depths that claimed her life. The story of haunted Pulpit Rock, and the long disappearance, death and discovery of Mabel is a tale that is sad, creepy and odd.

Mabel Smith Douglass went out from Camp Onondaga on Lake Placid on a solo rowboat trip on September 21, 1933, and was not seen until her corpse was pulled from the dark depths on September 15, 1963. Her body was nestled on the silty lake bottom at a depth of one hundred feet. Her family was closing the camp that day before heading back to New Jersey. Mabel was an accomplished woman, having been the first dean of the New Jersey College for Women at Rutgers. Her life was filled with tragedy, as her

The ominous and beautiful Pulpit Rock overlooking the black waters on Lake Placid. *Author's collection.*

husband had died, and her son committed suicide. The lady of the lake had become depressed, because on top of the family horror, she also encountered professional troubles. Mabel Smith Douglass had a nervous breakdown and spent a year in a mental health facility before being released and brought to the family camp in Lake Placid. Years after Mabel disappeared to the bottom of the lake and her death was ruled a suicide, her daughter Edith also suffered a mental breakdown and killed herself.

A couple of practicing scuba divers found Mabel's body thirty years after her death. It was 12:45 p.m. on September 15, 1963, when members of the Lake Champlain Wreck Raiders Diving Club took the appropriately named boat *Sea Witch* out to Pulpit Rock to explore possible caves in the deep water. The two divers, James Rogers and Richard Niffenegger, were down at the bottom when, in the over-one-hundred-foot depths, they saw what looked like a wax dummy sitting there. They thought it couldn't have been a human body, as it was perfect in its appearance—a perfect mannequin lying on the floor of the lake. It was lying on its side, legs crouched, with a rope tied around its neck that was attached to a boat anchor. James grabbed Mabel's

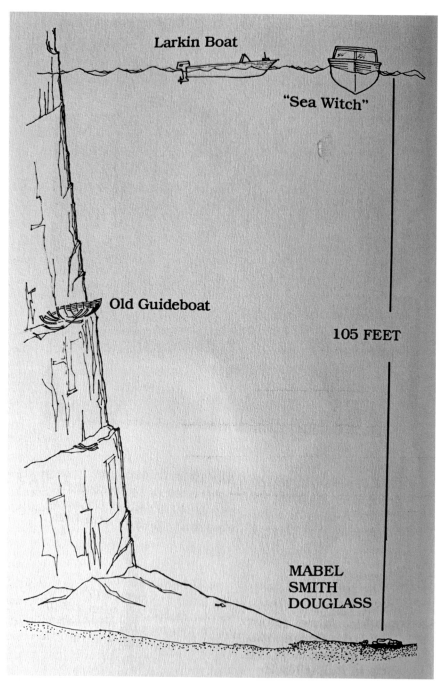

Larkin Boat

"Sea Witch"

Old Guideboat

105 FEET

MABEL
SMITH
DOUGLASS

An illustration of the body recovery at Pulpit Rock. *From* A Lady in the Lake, *by George Christian Ortloff.*

arm, and it came right off. The men knew it was a dead body. James stayed down while Richard surfaced and yelled to the crew of the *Sea Witch*, "We found a body!" He dove back down, and as the men cradled Mabel and started to bring her up, chunks of her face fell off until it was just her skull. The men tried not to vomit in their masks as the perfect dead body became a gruesome corpse.

When they got to the surface and Mabel's body hit the air, more of her dead flesh melted off. The men in the water and in the boat looked on in horror and gasped in shock at what they witnessed. They decided not to do anything else until the police got there. They waved down the *Doris*, a tourist boat filled with gawking onlookers. They left to get the police. A wake hit the body, and Mabel's head came off. They were able to save it, although her jaw came loose and was lost. They put a beach towel under her remains and held them in place until the police boat arrived to haul the long-missing woman to the coroner's office for examination. The coroner removed fishing line and several lures that had become embedded in the body. Although Mabel had a rope and anchor tied around her neck, her death was ruled a suicide. The coroner described her skin as feeling like cold wax and rock hard. Her complexion looked like pure ivory, paler than a typical corpse. There was no bloat, no discoloring, no smell and no decomposition. The coroner reasoned that Mabel's body had been preserved because the deep water never got above 34° Fahrenheit, and the lack of current and flesh-eating aquatic animals left her body undisturbed for thirty years.

Her body may have left the comfortable depths next to Pulpit Rock, but her spirit remained. Mabel had no living relatives, and her body was taken to Brooklyn, where she was buried with her husband and children. The legend in the area says that Pulpit Rock had been used by the Natives as a burial place; they'd throw their dead loved ones off the top and into the deep waters. That may be a legend, but Mabel's sad ending is not, and the legend of her spirit grew, as many campers and boaters have claimed to see her spirit floating above the waters next to Pulpit Rock.

The Lake Placid Boat Tour is the only way for the curious to observe Pulpit Rock, as there is no public launch and recreational jet skis are not allowed. Only those who own camps can boat around the dark waters of Lake Placid, so unless you know a lakeside resident with a boat, you must buy your ticket and board the pontoon boat with your friendly tour guide to take you around. You'll see all the grand camps along the way, and Pulpit Rock is on your last pass before returning to the dock. The cliff juts out, ominous and brooding, with flecks of pines along its balding edge. They named it Pulpit Rock because it looks as if a preacher could conduct a sermon from the top.

I went to Lake Placid on a sunny July day, not realizing it was the Ironman weekend. Thousands of the world's best athletes were running, stretching and biking around every square inch on the village and surrounding areas, yet none bought a ticket to ride the pontoon boat. Little did they know of the tragedy and ghost so close to their training and competition. I was mixed in with the other soft, middle-aged adventurers and curious touristy breed, their cellphones plastered to their indifferent noses. Captain Tom Mason was our driver and our verbal guide to the best Lake Placid had to offer. He was fun, pleasant and made the tour entertaining and educational. Captain Tom talked about the tragedy as we pulled closer to Pulpit Rock. I felt sad as he described Mabel's demise and the recovery of her body. The water was calm and dark on that sunny day. Pulpit Rock was large and loomed over as we went past. I wondered why Mabel would stay at the spot of her death. Many ghosts stick to places of love or reverence—not a sad, wet, suicidal rock lagoon. Perhaps her spirit is longing for her lost son and husband. The next time I go on the Lake Placid tour with Captain Tom, I'll be sure to place flowers on the spot of the death of the remarkable Mabel Smith Douglass, where her tormented spirit floats forever.

SAGAMORE RESORT
BOLTON LANDING

On the banks of Lake George, on an island in the town of Bolton Landing, is one of top-ten most haunted hotels in the United States. The Sagamore Resort is so filled with ghosts, they practically outnumber the living guests who come and go from this majestic resort that's had its share of tragedy since it first opened in 1883. The hotel burned down multiple times, with fires occurring in 1893 and 1914. The hotel resort was rebuilt in the early 1920s and again in 1930. Even though the hotel made it through the Great Depression, it was closed in 1981 due to hard times. Norman Wolgin purchased the Sagamore and restored it to its former grandeur. The ghosts have been there all along, waiting for more guests to entertain them from in afterlife. The hotel sits on spirited land that has been called a Native burial ground. The island and the entire region on and around Lake George hosted many battles throughout the eighteenth century that included the

The Sagamore Resort is world-renowned for its hospitality and numerous ghosts. *Author's collection.*

British, French and the local Native tribes. The Sagamore Resort is a large, luxurious hotel that is amazing in its beauty and sits on an island against a beautiful view of Lake George. It's no wonder the ghosts love sticking around, as the other side cannot match the earthbound beauty of the jewel of the Adirondacks: the Sagamore.

The ghosts and hauntings of the Sagamore Resort are very active, with many spooky tales from staff and guests. There's Lillian, the ghost in her early twenties who appears in a puce-colored dress and who's always seen standing on an open porch, looking down on the lake. The guest services elevator is host to a ghost named Walter, who wears, for all eternity, a brown three-piece suit and sports a walrus mustache. A young boy was hit and killed by a car on the grounds in the 1950s, and his spirit has been seen by many, hanging around the golf course. Not all ghosts are scary or grumpy, as the golf course ghost boy is rather jolly in the afterlife. The mischievous little boy ghost steals golf balls and then flings them at other golfers on the course. His ghostly giggles are heard constantly while he's playing his haunted pranks. He's not the only child entity, however, as there have been sightings of other ghost children laughing and running the hallways of the resort.

Guest sightings have included a woman in white whose spirit hovers over sleeping guests. These guests have awakened to her blowing her ghostly cold mist breath on their eyelids. A female ghost wearing a blue polka dot dress has also been seen leisurely strolling the Sagamore's hallways and restaurant. And a ghost couple has been witnessed, fighting for all eternity. Guests have witnessed the quarreling spirits repeat their fight that ends in him throwing her to the floor. She reaches for him and fades away. This is a residual haunting, as it's a repeat in which the same event happens over and over, like a broken record. If it were an intelligent haunting, the ghosts would interact and react to the guests. The Sagamore Resort is overstuffed with both types of hauntings and many more tales of the haunted.

It was a crisp, cold January day when I visited the Sagamore Resort and brought along my son Jakob Webster. The drive up to the Sagamore Resort is a winding beauty, and the spooky road slithers along the topography of the banks of Lake George. Bolton Landing is a picturesque tourist town, but it was when I was driving by the Sembrich Opera Museum and Music Venue that I halted my truck and stared at a beautiful structure that looked as haunted as any building I had ever viewed. I sallied forth, and as I was crossing the little bridge that brought us to the island that hosts the Sagamore Resort, there was a man on a bicycle with a prominent black eye patch. I knew we were in a magical place. When I pulled up, my breath was taken away by the resort's beauty and grandeur. My son said, "Wow, look at this place, Dad." I got the odd feeling I get when I'm on a hot ghost hunt when I pulled up and parked. The wind was whipping off of Lake George, and the air was crisp and fresh. We walked the perimeter of the grand resort. There was no one else on the lake's perimeter as I took photographs and we admired the stunning Sagamore. I could see why it was haunted. I'd certainly love to make it the final place my ghost would haunt.

Jake and I walked into the lobby and approached the front desk, where we were greeted by a friendly receptionist who gave me a list of ghosts in the resort and called the resident expert to give us a private ghost tour. It was a trippy paranormal walk we will never forget. Our haunted adventure started with meeting Shawnee Black, who works in the Sagamore Resort Spa but who is also the person who guides visitors to the haunted locations. Shawnee said she sees ghosts and was raised in a funeral home. She was very friendly and eager to show us the ghosts. It started with a ride in the haunted elevator. Shawnee said that many people see a full-bodied apparition in the elevator

Left: An odd elevator mirror at the Sagamore Resort. *Author's collection.*

Right: Jake Webster with a ghost meter at the Sagamore Resort. *Author's collection.*

and that most freak out at the odd mirrors that are on both sides. Indeed, Jake and I looked into the elevator mirror, and a very strange repetition of us to infinity was created there, like a mirage.

It was at this point of wonderment that we felt a strange feeling, and the ghost meters went haywire. I had given Jake two meters. One was a mel meter that measures temperature and electromagnetism, and the other was a gauss meter. They were both going off, which indicated to us there was a ghostly presence. I had a strong feeling that the haunted elevator was a portal that the ghosts were using to travel from their realm to ours, and Shawnee agreed. The elevator door opened, and we walked out into an area that was outside a kitchen where random items were stored. Shawnee said most people do not see this area. On many occasions, she and the staff had seen a ghost hanging around in this spot. I had to admit that the spot creeped me out, and Jake was rather silent. My son is a skeptic and doesn't believe in ghosts, but his viewpoint was put to the test—but not until the end of the tour.

While we walked with Shawnee, she spun the tales of the ghosts that are talked about the most. She said that, back in 2003, there was a sous chef preparing food at 4:30 a.m. and playing music from the rapper

Eminem on the radio. The beats were blasting when the chef looked up and saw a woman in her thirties, wearing a light-green gown from Depression-era fashion. She gestured to the radio with a curious look and said, "Whose words are these?" She then walked through the wall. The chef picked up his knives, rolled them in their canvas carrying case and walked out of the kitchen and the Sagamore Resort. Shawnee talked about the time a hotel manager was alone at the front desk at 1:45 a.m. when the elevator opened and a woman in Victorian garb walked out, said nothing and passed through a wall. Then she told us of a time when two employees were working the front desk late at night and the ghosts of a man and a woman dressed in early twentieth century–style clothing came around the corner and asked about the party in the ballroom. There was no party, and they walked away and disappeared as they moved. The Sagamore Resort also has a Native ghost that has been seen walking the courtyard by the water, and there's a ghost that's always seen sitting and playing cards. The ghosts are playful, Shawnee says, and constantly flush the toilets in the spa. They always make their paranormal flush when the water closets are empty.

Shawnee saved the best ghost for last by talking about the legend of the murdered maid. A female employee was murdered in a room on the second floor in the 1930s and can now be seen in her blue uniform dress. The maid had an affair with a resort guest and was fired. When she returned to the room, the man's wife arrived, and he confessed to having the affair. The wife went ballistic and fought with the maid; she smothered the maid to death with a pillow from the sinful bed. The couple fled and left the murdered maid on the floor. It was assumed the maid died of a heart attack when her cold body was found the next day. From then on, her angry ghost has been in the room and has been seen just outside the room in the hall.

I am a paranormal investigator and ghost hunter, so Shawnee asked me if she thought I could identify the room. I told her I'm an empath and sensitive to ghosts but that I am not psychic or a medium. I would try. Why not? I'm always up for a challenge. I gave my skeptic son the handheld ghost devices, and we all went to the second floor. The hallways are narrow and the ceilings are low on the second floor, and with the carpet pattern and yellowish lights, it has an odd, creepy, ghostly feel. There are multiple hallways that offshoot from a center hall. I looked at them, pointed and said, "It's down this hallway." Shawnee confirmed, so I started walking down the hall with her and Jakob behind me. I walked past about a dozen rooms when, all of a sudden, I got woozy, and my stomach felt like I had been gut punched. I turned and placed my hands on the door and said, "This is the room, right?" Shawnee confirmed it, and I was amazed I identified the room. Jakob walked over and placed the ghost meters by the door, and they went off, full blast. We could not go into the room, as it had a guest. The Sagamore Resort lives up to its title of being one of the most haunted hotels in the United States. The beauty of the place is accented by the gorgeous and lavish ghosts that call the Sagamore their eternal home.

MERRILL MAGEE INN
WARRENSBURG

Sometimes, a love or worldly fondness of a building can lead to a ghost sticking around and haunting a place that they adored when they lived in an earthbound body. The Merrill Magee Inn was a pleasant paranormal experience wrapped around a loving innkeeper by the name of Daniel DelGaudio. The Merrill Magee Inn was built as a farmhouse for Stephen Griffing in 1833 and had a second story added in the 1850s and a wing added in the early twentieth century. Griffing's granddaughter Grace Merrill Lown Magee was the last of the family to occupy the home. She lived well into her nineties and passed away in 1979, with tales of her ghost haunting the building. The inn was purchased 2014 by Michael and Donna Flanagan, along with Michael's brother Richard and his wife, Leslie Flanagan. The inn has seen a lot of renovation and is a cornerstone of Warrensburg, as it's in the National Register of Historic Places.

I spent a wonderful evening in the main inn on a ghost hunting trip in the middle of the July heat. I went into the inn building, where the guest rooms are located, and met Daniel DelGauido, who had worked for many years at the Merrill Magee Inn and who has an impressive background and experience as an innkeeper. I gave him my ghost card and introduced myself as a paranormal investigator and author. I wanted to hear the tales of the haunted inn, and he was more than happy to accommodate me. The building that is separated and close to the front of the property is the location Daniel felt was most haunted. This is where the pub, restaurant, kitchen and second-floor offices are located.

Daniel asked if I was a clairvoyant or psychic. I told him no, that, if anything, I'm an empath with a tidbit of ability to tune into the

The beauty of the Merrill Magee Inn makes the ghosts happy. *Author's collection.*

paranormal realm. Many years of being a member of the Ghost Seekers of Central New York has built my medium mind muscles, so I can get ghost interaction or detect the paranormal. He said he'd walk me through and not say anything. It was a test, and that's OK, as going into a place cold can be a lot of fun. Many paranormal investigators and mediums embrace this approach. Daniel walked me through the entire structure, including both floors, and when I walked into the pub area, I halted as I became lit up. I said, "Wow," as I held up both of my arms and showed Daniel that every hair was standing straight up, both arms awash with goosebumps. He smiled and said his back was ice cold. He said nothing else as we descended into the basement. It was lovely, and I enjoyed it, but my ghostly buzz had worn off. We walked back upstairs, and when

I walked into the bar area, the same paranormal experience happened. I asked Daniel if this was the area the ghosts haunted most. I felt it was the spiritual epicenter of the Merrill Magee Inn, and Daniel nodded and agreed. Yes, I had found the ghost hot spot.

Daniel mentioned that the area was especially active when the bar was being remodeled, as that area was the original part of the homestead over 180 years ago. I nodded a yes, as that is very common. I don't know why ghost activity picks up during remodeling. My theory is that their spirit is ingrained into the structure, and the remodeling stirs them up. Daniel mentioned that a ghost hunting group had done an investigation and found nothing, but I explained this is not an exact science; there's no such thing as paranormal on demand (POD). Ghost hunting is a pursuit and calling for many, but even the most gifted mediums cannot conjure or force spirits to appear. They work on their own times and reasons only known to themselves. Daniel asked me if it could be a contemporary ghost, a modern spirit. I said, "Of course." It's funny how people think every ghost is like something out of movie, wearing a top hat and tails, lathered in chains, carrying a candelabra and groaning. Well, you can have that, but ghosts can be the spirits of the recently departed. Daniel felt that it could be the spirit of an owner who had recently passed away. This gentleman loved the Merrill Magee Inn and lovingly worked with his own hands in the remodeling. I told Daniel that it makes perfect sense for a spirit to stay at the place they loved.

There is no doubt that the Merrill Magee Inn is haunted by the spirit of a man who adored the structure, as you can feel the love, warmth and pride. During your visit, sit in the bar area, hold up your beverage and toast to the spirit who's pleased you're there, sharing your smiles.

THE MYSTERY SPOT OF LAKE GEORGE
LAKE GEORGE

If you go to one place in this book, you must visit the strange, odd and spooky mystery spot of Lake George. I went and stood on the spot and experienced a haunted vocal experience that one could only describe as being from another dimension. I had my son Jakob as my traveling companion, and he was freaked out and astounded at the anomaly that is the mystery spot of Lake George. There are theories that ghosts and

Author and paranormal investigator Dennis Webster experiences the oddball anomaly of the Lake George Mystery Spot. *Author's collection.*

shadow people exist in another dimension, another plane of existence, and that we can only slightly feel or experience it as a paranormal tickle. Some scientists believe that when we experience déjà vu, we are rubbing up against a multiverse. Albert Einstein's theory of relativity just might explain the ghostly mystery spot. In his theory, space and time are part of a continuum called space-time. Space has three dimensions, with the fourth dimension being time. But, recently, scientists have declared there must be extra dimensions we cannot perceive. I would say the mystery spot might just be a fifth dimension, where a portal or a gateway to the realm of the dead or a wait station for the living to experience another dimension is located. How else can one explain standing in the center of the spot, yelling at the top of your lungs and hearing an odd tinny sound in response. It's as if your soul is trapped inside the dimension where an invisible bubble reflects your sounds back in an odd paranormal tinge. Local Native legend states that the spot was where an ancient god called Katchalototail appeared to shout his wisdom across Lake George. Perhaps he was a traveler from a multiverse or another dimension, and the mystery spot anomaly is the residual paranormal energy that was left over from his holy visit.

You can find the mystery spot by going behind the Lake George Visitor Center. There, you'll see a circular platform with a painted blue map of Lake George with a metal compass etched into it. In the exact center, you must stand where the X marks the spot. You must face the lake and talk or shout and be prepared for a paranormal experience. Another strange fact is if you are very tall, the anomaly doesn't work, so you must kneel down. This shows that the spot has an invisible bubble that you must be inside of to get the mystery experience. Try it, and you will not be disappointed with your experience of being a ghost while still a part of our solid flesh world.

SKENE MANOR
WHITEHALL

Nestled on a steep hill, Skene Manor juts out as the beautiful watcher of all of Whitehall, yet her grand look hosts ghosts. The town is known nationally as a hotbed of Bigfoot sightings and for its gatherings of all fans of the hairy creature, yet Whitehall has a grand dame of a mansion that stands haunted and majestic among the steep hills. Skene Manor is a Victorian Gothic Revival home that was built in 1874 by Supreme Court justice Joseph H. Potter, and it was a private residence until 1946, when it was converted into a restaurant. In 1995, Whitehall Skene Manor Preservation Inc. purchased the mansion. The gorgeous Skene Manor was placed in the National Register of Historic Places in 1959. The manor has all sorts of legends and rumors that have been put on it, along with tales of the place being haunted.

The manor sits on land that was owned by Phillip Skene, the founder of Whitehall. The town was originally called Skenesborough. Skene Manor's original name was "Mountain Terrace" and was built at a cost of $25,000. It was constructed from gray sandstone that was quarried from Skene Mountain by stonecutters from Italy. I read that the manor was haunted by the ghost of Mrs. Skene, who is said to have been buried in the basement. That was not true, and I got the real story from Richard Brewer, the docent at Skene Manor. I had heard about the beauty of Skene Manor and was agog at it in person. Getting to it is not an easy task, and GPS systems

get discombobulated. The route through the town and up the steep hill is cramped, but the payoff is worth it, as you come around a steep bend and the manor pops right out like a grand gray dame.

It was a beautiful blue-sky day, and the sunbeams glistened off the manor, making it shine through the green foliage that surrounded it. I walked the grounds and was in awe. I went inside and met Richard, who was about to perform a tour. He talked with me about Katharine Skene. She was buried

Opposite: Skene Manor is the supermodel of mansions. Oh, and it has ghosts. *Author's collection.*

Right: The ghost of Skene Manor favors the library on the second floor. *Author's collection.*

by her husband, Philip, in a lead coffin in her home, but it was another mansion in town, not Skene Manor. It was sad to hear that, during the Revolutionary War, American Patriots removed Katherine and melted down her lead casket to make musket balls and cannon balls. The soldiers felt bad and reburied her on the grounds. Rumors swirled that it was Katherine's ghost haunting Skene Manor, but neither she nor her husband ever lived there. There was something paranormal going on in the manor, as I would discover soon enough.

I was able to go along with a few other people as Richard gave the grand tour, walking us room to room and going into great detail on the history of the manor and the people who had lived there. His knowledge was vast and filled with love and enthusiasm. I waited until the end of the tour, and Richard told me some of the ghost stories. He said a local ghost group had investigated the manor and had some fascinating evidence. I didn't have the details of that, as it was kept private, but I could feel the spirits while I was on the tour.

I was allowed to wander Skene Manor of my own free will, except for the basement that was somehow blocked from all, including ghost hunting teams that had investigated the manor. Still, it was an honor and a privilege to be able to go through the floors and rooms alone. I went up into the crow's nest, peered out and gasped at the gorgeous hilltop view of breathtaking scenery. It was up there that I sat in solace, closed my eyes and spoke to the spirits. I felt something coming up the spiral staircase, yet it stopped short, and I could not get it to come closer. I felt it was a female ghost, but she was shy and would not come closer or tell me her name. I sat for quite a while, then got up and descended when I could tell the she had left.

As I wandered around, I tended to be drawn into the handful of rooms that were not finished; some had remnants of remodeling construction debris, along with some randomly stored items. I felt nothing paranormal in these rooms as I wandered, but I was drawn into the library on the second floor that had an old writing desk with a manual typewriter. Being a writer, I was drawn to the desk as a moth is drawn to a flickering fire. I opened up my journal and began to write random thoughts of Skene Manor when I heard soft footsteps coming down the hall. They were what I would refer to as belonging to a female and dainty, not the clodhoppers or pounding steps that male ghosts put forth. The female ghost's footsteps were coming from just outside the room I was in. I stopped, as I knew I was all alone up there; the tour group I had been with was finished and had departed. There were volunteers, but all of them, along with Richard, were in the first-floor kitchen and foyer. I set my pen down as the steps got closer and louder. I leapt from my chair and sprinted out into the hall, expecting to catch a random person wandering like myself, yet no one was there. It had to be the female ghost from earlier, up in the turret. I said to the spirit, "Don't be shy. I mean no harm."

I went back into the library, sat down and wrote of what had just happened, and I said aloud something I had never said in all my life: "I love you." I was compelled to confess to a female ghost who I had not seen or met, but I knew she was there. I was telling the library in Skene Manor that I adored it, not a beautiful mortal earthbound enchantress, a prancing white poodle or a toasted buttered raisin bagel on a plate—nope, I loved the female ghost. I loved the library. I loved Skene Manor. I was compelled to say it as I felt her spirit walking down the hall to observe a hewer of words sitting at the instrument that hosts such pursuits and lovingly jotting in a journal. I had my digital recorder going and picked up clear footsteps, so my paranormal experience was verified. I imagined that the ghost that had interacted with me watched Whitehall from the turret window, as the view was astounding and vast. I couldn't verify who the female ghost was. I will return to Skene Manor, and perhaps she will show herself to me and tell me her name.

RHINELANDER ESTATE
SPECULATOR

The burned-out remains of the Rhinelander Estate are still haunted to this day. Deep within the woods, along a gravel road that cars not dare tread, is the spot where the sad entity of a lonely, sequestered, beautiful spirit wanders her isolated spot for all eternity, waiting for visitors to cheer her up. This was the saddest and loneliest place I visited on all my paranormal travels for *Haunted Adirondacks*. The story is one of a captive beauty, a jealous husband and the sadness that can occur, even within the beauty of the mountain woods.

The remnants of the foundation of the burned-down nineteenth-century Rhinelander Estate. *Author's collection.*

Canoe trip to Elm Lake. The Rhinelander mansion was built on the hillside in 1805.

An Elm Lake canoe trip in close proximity of the Rhinelander Estate. *Courtesy of the Lake Pleasant Public Library.*

This is the haunted tale of Phillip Rhinelander Jr. and his wife, Mary. They moved to Lake Pleasant in 1815 and cleared a large plot that overlooked Elm Lake. Phillip was a founding father of Lake Pleasant and Speculator. He served in many roles in the area, including town supervisor, commissioner of schools, election inspector and many more. The Rhinelanders were part of a prominent family who built a mansion in the woods that also had a stable, barn and servants' quarters. Life may have looked great from the outside, but the legend of their love and the stories surrounding them are fascinating and tragic. It was said that Phillip was a very jealous man and that Mary was a stunning beauty who had to live a lonely life, as he kept her sequestered in the Rhinelander mansion, away from the peering eyes of men. The mansion was very remote, and Mary was not allowed to go into town unless under the supervision of Phillip, but for the majority of her time, she was held prisoner in her mansion on the hill. His jealousy even held when it came to Mary's family and friends, as he would take her handwritten letters to them from her and never send them. She was cut off from contact with anybody.

The legends and rumors swirled, as it's said that she befriended a peddler who disappeared under mysterious circumstances. Some say Phillip murdered the man and threw him down the well on the property. It was also said that servants were murdered, with one found floating along the shoreline of Elm Lake. These legends are hard to verify; however, there is no doubt that a lonely woman was kept hostage in a beautiful mansion in the thick Adirondack wilderness, far from her hometown of New York City.

Mary died at the Rhinelander Estate in 1818, with rumors swirling that is was due to her husband poisoning her. My thoughts are that she could've died from loneliness and a broken heart. Phillip built a stone vault in the mansion and placed her body there; it was eventually relocated by her family to New York City. Phillip left Speculator and Lake Pleasant in 1823 and passed away in 1830. The estate had caretakers for years, who claimed that Mary's spirit would visit them when they were asleep in her old bedroom. One caretaker woke to her ghost sitting in the room and sobbing, while another resident in the mansion saw her spirit sitting in the room and stroking her hair. Many times, the sound of Phillip's boots stomping up and down the stairs could be heard. Caretakers' children would comment on candles flying in the air.

The mansion was later abandoned and boarded up, yet throughout the nineteenth century, the townspeople visited the haunted mansion to see the ghost of Mary looking out of the second-story window. Some commented that they could hear a child crying from inside the empty estate. The Rhinelander Estate succumbed to age and arson when it burned to the ground in 1875. The haunted legends grew, and campers would sleep overnight within the foundation's walls to hear footsteps, see an entity floating in the woods and get an overwhelming feeling of sadness.

I decided to visit the ruins of the Rhinelander Estate in the middle of July, as I was drawn to the legends and the sadness of a beautiful ghost in the form of Mary. I called Anne Weaver, a Lake Pleasant historian who was kind enough to put me in contact with her son Aaron Weaver, the expert on the Rhinelander Estate. He has written about the estate and has taken visitors to the ruins of the mansion. I drove up the winding Route 8, which took me deep into the heart of the Adirondacks; it got more beautiful the farther north I drove, with tall pines hugging both sides of the road. The town of Speculator and Lake Pleasant were charming and gorgeous. I stopped in at the Lake Pleasant Library and talked with Sherry Matthews, the director, who was very friendly and spent time talking to me about the Rhinelanders. I stopped by where Aaron worked, the Charlie Johns Supermarket, and he was kind enough to take a quick break to give me directions to the estate. The estate is on New York State land, but you can visit it during the day.

It was around noon, sunny and very hot. One would think ghosts only come out during cold, dark and stormy nights, but I was soon to have my most haunted daytime encounter in all my paranormal travels. I had a great talk with Aaron, and I felt the passion and respect he has for the history and the site of Mary's sad spirit. He explained that it was on a dirt road at the end of a paved road and that I might have to walk, as it is rough terrain for a car. I was fortunate, as I had my four-wheel drive pickup truck, but Aaron was correct; it was bumpy going, but luck was on my side, as there had been a long, hot stretch in July, and the dirt road was dry and solid. The trek was at least two miles into the deep woods and up some steep hills; my teeth chattered from bouncing. There was no way a car could've made that route.

I pulled up to the spot that was designated by a small blue-and-yellow marker that had been erected by the Historical Society of Lake Pleasant and Speculator. The sun blazed on my neck, and I sipped water while leaning against my truck. I had my handheld ghost meter and my digital recorder with me. I walked into the woods, and the shade from the thick trees downgraded the brightness and reduced the temperature. As I walked into the woods, I halted and marveled at the quiet beauty. Rarely does one get to be isolated, miles from population and the noise of the citizenry. All I could hear was the rustling of the leaves as the wind walked through with its simple song. The foundation walls were covered with bright-green overgrowth. I could feel the air and vibe change as I stepped over the wall and onto the hallowed ground of what was left of the Rhinelander Estate. There was no cellar, just a filled-in area that had several inches of wall jutting up. I could easily make out the shape of the mansion and strolled the perimeter, looking for a place to sit. I was drawn to the far-left corner in the back, so I sat and placed my legs out in front of me.

I started asking about Mary—if she was there. All of a sudden, the sweet smell of the Adirondack woods was replaced with a foul odor. Then the wind ceased, and there was complete silence. The birds weren't even chirping, and the squirrels stopped shuffling through the underbrush. I closed my eyes, and all of a sudden, I heard a female voice behind me. I couldn't make out what she was saying, as it was a whisper a good twenty feet behind me. When it stopped, I opened my eyes, turned around and looked, but no one was there. I got up and walked through the interior of the walls, and I started to speak to the spirit of Phillip, asking if he loved Mary. I said that I read she was very beautiful. I halted, as I got very sad, and my right eye started to itch and have a pain for no apparent reason. My heart started to race, and depression came in a wave over me. I decided to lie down in the middle of the ruins and meditate. I lay flat on my back, crossed my legs at the ankles and clasped my hands on my chest. I was looking up, toward the trees, and the leaves were so thick that I couldn't see the bright sun through them. I closed my eyes and started my Yoga Nidra. I was getting myself into a trance when I heard footsteps coming from behind me. I did not dare to open my eyes. The footsteps were light and slow and stopped about a foot behind my head. I felt it was the spirit of Mary, looking at me with curiosity. I was probably the only person to lie down flat and meditate, so I'm sure my mortal pose came across as curious and odd. I just knew she didn't want me looking at her. I had the feeling she was worried about Phillip's ghost getting jealous if I looked at her. It was at this point that I couldn't believe my ears, as I heard a loud pig grunt from my left. It was quiet, then I heard a second one. My handheld ghost meter started to go off, and when it stopped, I knew Mary was gone. I opened my eyes, sat up and looked around, but there was no person or pig—nothing.

The wind started back up, and the leaves started rustling. I got up and walked over to where the pig grunts had come from, and it was outside the ruins. My guess is that it was a residual haunt of a pig in a pen from long ago. The ghost of Mary, however, was intelligent, as she was there. The sadness that enveloped me disappeared as soon as I stepped across the property line and back out to the dirt road. I leaned against my truck for quite a while, drinking a bottle of water in the July heat, and I stared at the ruins of the Rhinelander Estate. My heart broke for the sad and lonely Mary who was still trapped up on the Adirondack hill, far away from her friends and loved ones. I said a prayer, hoping her soul would move on to where she could find friendship, joy and love.

THE BIGFOOT OF OHIO
OHIO

Many residents and forest rangers in the town of Ohio and nearby Woodgate have seen or heard the tales of those who have been frightened by the sight Bigfoot wandering through the thick Adirondack pine forests. Most people would think of the northwestern area of the United States as the only place where Bigfoot resides; however, these monsters have been seen in the

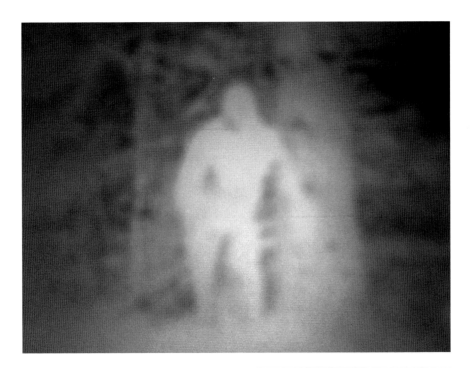

Above: Bigfoot captured on a trail camera in the town of Ohio. *Courtesy of Jeff Gee and Matt Rothwell.*

Right: Whitehall hosts an annual celebration of its Bigfoot infamy. *Author's collection.*

A Bigfoot statue in the town of Whitehall. *Author's collection.*

Adirondacks for hundreds of years or as long as humans have been walking the footpaths of the big beasts. I spoke to a New York State forest ranger who asked not to be identified, but he did tell me that he had seen Bigfoot in the Ohio area of the Adirondacks. He chuckled, and when I asked what was so funny, he replied, "We just got a new ranger up here. Wait until they see one of these furry giants. Then we'll know if they're cut out to be patrolling in these woods." I smiled back and nodded. I can't imagine the panic and terror someone must feel when they eyewitness an eight-foot-tall anthropoid hairy creature with foul breath and a skunk-like stench.

The Adirondacks have been host to this mysterious paranormal creature since before the White man came to this country, and the Natives referred to this creature as Sasquatch. Of course, Bigfoot can exist in the Adirondacks, as the park has a dense forest, limited human population and millions of pristine acres. But is Bigfoot part of the paranormal? Yes, the story of the Adirondack Bigfoot belongs in a haunted book, as there are theories that this creature could be a traveler between other dimensions or multiverses. It makes sense when you think about how they appear and disappear and the lack of physical evidence, like scat or corpses of the dead beasts. Could the Bigfoot have the ability to enter our realm through portals?

No matter their origin or method of travel, they are intimidating and scary to small, soft humans. How scared would you be if you ran into a Bigfoot while hiking on a remote trail? I would say very scared and haunted is one way you can put it. Bigfoot has been witnessed in Saranac Lake, and there have been massive amounts of sightings in Whitehall. The most Bigfoot sightings, by far, have occurred in the vicinity of Whitehall. The town embraces its notoriety on the subject, as it hosts a Sasquatch festival every fall that includes guest speakers, experts on the topic, food, music and a Bigfoot calling contest. When I stopped in town to visit Skene Manor, I stopped by the Skenesborough Museum and spoke to the curator, who lovingly spoke of the hairy beasts the town was famous for.

Whitehall is such a beautiful spot that one can see why Bigfoot would hang around. The town was also the birthplace of the U.S. Navy and played a huge part in the United States gaining its independence, with naval battles led by Benedict Arnold launching from there. When the French explorer Samuel de Champlain came to America in 1603 and saw the region, he was told by the Natives of the "gougou," a hairy giant that would frighten them. They told Champlain of the beast hissing and throwing rocks at them. There have been many sightings of the gougou in the Adirondacks, including in 1996, when two men were canoeing on Pine Pond at dusk and saw what they thought was a bear along the tree line. They paddled closer, and the hairy monster stood up and ran off into the woods with the quickness of a mountain lion. There was a famous sighting at Saranac Lake, where a lady who was driving her car came across what she thought was a bear lying in the middle of the road. She stopped, and as it stood up on two legs, she realized it was not a bear but a Bigfoot. The enraged beast apparently tore the door off of her car before bolting into the woods.

This takes me to a firsthand story told to me by a friend and former coworker, Matt Rothwell. He approached me and asked about my being a ghost hunter and into the paranormal. He had a picture on his cellphone that had been captured on a trail camera by his friend Jeff Gee. Matt told me that they had been off of Nellis Road in the Adirondack town of Ohio and had set up a camera on a tree in the hopes of capturing a black bear. They took a five-gallon pail, placed chunks of raw red meat in it and left it right where the camera would snap a picture. It had a night vision mode, so if a bear came into the area at night, they'd get a good picture. After a few days, they went back into the woods and found the five-gallon bucket still standing upright, yet all of the meat had been removed. They thought it odd, as a black bear would certainly have knocked the bucket over to get to the juicy morsels inside. They took down the trail camera, anticipating a great photograph of a black bear snacking on the bait. But what they got instead was a photograph of a large humanoid. It was not a bear and was too tall and large to be a human. The photograph was blurry and smudged, but there was no doubt that it was a Bigfoot. Matt showed me, and there is a tree behind the Bigfoot; they measured to the knot that was right next to its head and estimated it was eight feet tall. Looking at the picture, the beast is very thick in its trunk and extremities, with an estimated weight between four hundred and five hundred pounds. Many people have seen this photograph and are completely baffled by it—proof the Adirondack Bigfoot exists. The next time you go up Route 8 and into the town of Ohio, be aware of the hairy beasts, not the ones hanging out in the Ohio Tavern, but the eight-foot-tall, stinky, woods walker variety Bigfoot.

SOUTHERN ADIRONDACK GENERAL STORE AND CAFÉ
STRATFORD

On the bottom edge of the Adirondack territorial blue line sits a quiet and down-home place that hosts shoppers, diners and ghosts. The Southern Adirondack General Store and Café has a male entity named John who roams around and greets visitors; he also loves to interact with the owners, Cheryl Osterhout-Dayter and her husband, Steve Dayter. The place is filled with the scent of great food, laughter and love, so it's easy to see why spirits like John would want to hang around. Steve and Cheryl have had many interactions with the friendly male spirit overseer, but they have also encountered a little girl ghost dashing from the kitchen and into the back

The Southern Adirondack General Store and Café with "John" the ghost in the window. *Photograph by Josh Aust.*

storeroom. The owners have a photograph that shows the ghost of John standing by the front door—or at least where the door used to be. You can see through the ghost and see the posts and walls through him. The Ghost Seekers of Central New York analyzed the photograph and deemed it genuine and of the paranormal. The group's opinion is that the photograph is either a portal that ghosts use to travel back and forth from the paranormal plane to our plane or that it's a time slip, a snapshot of another time, when John was alive, and the door in the photograph was still in its old location.

The building was constructed in the 1860s and was originally called the Service House, run by Minnie Service. The two-story structure housed rugged Adirondack lumberjacks who were looking for a warm meal and cold brew after lengthy days of hacking trees. The second floor was allegedly a brothel, another kind of service that Minnie's place offered. The ghosts come out to play with Cheryl and Steve on a regular basis, including one saying "dad" while Steve was cooking, moving cans and tools around, moving a red basket and playing hide-and-seek. There was a tragic accident in the 1970s, when a young girl who was standing outside of the café was shot in the head by a person driving by in a car. The crime was never solved, but perhaps it's her spirit that haunts the building.

The Ghost Seekers of Central New York team, comprising Bernadette Peck, David Peck, Josh Aust, Len Bragg, Ed Livingston, Mark Webster and Liz Bridgman, was there to conduct an investigation. Dennis Webster was there, representing the Fort Schuyler Paranormal Society. It was a cool, clear Saturday night in October, with a full moon beaming down on the paranormal proceedings. Cheryl and Steve had the group arrive there in the late afternoon and purchased pizza so that the group could sit down with them and talk ghosts. There was a lot of good discussion, and there were smiles across the board; the team looked in amazement as they reviewed the spooky photograph Steve had of John the ghost. During this time, Josh was outside, snapping random photographs, and he picked up a shadow figure in the front window. It is a rare thing to capture, a full body entity during the daytime. It wasn't long before the darkness descended, and the team formed their circle. Bernadette Peck said the opening prayer:

St. Michael, the archangel, defend us in battle. Be our protection against the wickedness and snares of the devil. May God rebuke him, we humbly pray. And do thou, Prince of the Heavenly Hosts, by the divine power of God, cast into Hell Satan and all evil spirits who roam about the world, seeking the ruin of souls. Amen.

Above: Built in the late nineteenth century, the Service House hosted hardworking lumberjacks for chow, drinks and female relations on the second-floor brothel. *Courtesy of the Southern Adirondack General Store and Café.*

Left: A time warp ghostly portal shows the door that used to appear with a ghost in the foreground. *Courtesy of Cheryl Osterhout-Dayter and Steve Dayter.*

The teams broke into three groups, with one going into the basement, one in the main dining area and one in the back storage room. The ghosts were active right away, with the backroom being a hot spot, and Cheryl was in there as a mortal trigger object. The Ghost Seekers decided to keep both Cheryl and Steve as part of the investigation, as the spirits were familiar and friendly toward them. The investigation proved that the ghosts exist, with footsteps and groans coming from the back storeroom, and Cheryl got the name Georgia, a friend of hers who had passed. The team felt that the little girl ghost's name was Ellie and the male entity John. The team was able to capture voices talking in the basement, but the spookiest event occurred outside, near the area where the little girl was killed. There was an odd smell, and the team was drawn into the woods behind the café. The gauss meter and mel meter spiked in the woods, where there are no man-made electrical devices. There was something standing at the edge of the trees, and it hid from the team as we approached. It was curious and shy, but it was not a bad spirit. The team ended the night with a closing prayer and came away feeling relieved, for the café was full of fun, curious and playful ghosts who love the owners and the patrons very much. If you want a nice cup of coffee, great chow and a spiritual interaction, be sure to swing by the Southern Adirondack General Store and Café.

FOXY ROXY'S
POTSDAM

There's a place where you can get more than dessert with your tasty cheeseburger; at Foxy Roxy's, you can get a ghost on the side. The eatery is not a large place, but it is filled with paranormal activity. The Adirondack Park Paranormal Society (APPS) investigated the restaurant on a crisp, cold January evening. They went in with many known experiences from team member Marcy Brunet, who had been around the structure regularly and currently works within the building. Foxy Roxy's had been a family home for a number of years, and then, in the 1980s, it was a hair salon before it became a place that serves food. Marcy has the gift of the third eye where she can see, feel and hear the ghosts. She has had many interactions with the spirits at Foxy Roxy's, to the point where it's a normal part of her workday, although the ghosts do not collect a paycheck. She sees a tall, thin man with shaggy hair in the basement and a short, chubby male ghost in a Buffalo plaid shirt who is social and mingles among the diners. He likes to play pranks, like tapping Marcy on the shoulder or stroking her hair. One time, when Marcy was alone, after the place had closed, she was singing "Scottish Kilt" when she heard a male ghost singing along. Roxanne, the owner, has ghosts that follow her around. Roxy and Marcy like to say to these meddlesome spirits, "If you're not going to help, then go away." To Roxy and Marcy, the ghosts that reside in the restaurant are family.

The APPS team, comprising Aymee-Lynne Fisk, Brett Williamson, Jennifer Coriale, Christy Nier, Miranda Merrill, Marcy Brunet, Susan Goff, Damon Jacobs and Sarah Williamson, investigated the eatery in order to prove that the spooky tales and haunted experiences told by Marcy, Roxy and others were true. The squad of experienced paranormal investigators brought their equipment, including digital recorders, video cameras, rem pods and EMF meters, as well as dowsing rods and a pendulum. The greatest equipment is still the humanistic five senses, but in a pinch, with mechanical devices and feelings, you can certify a paranormal event and a haunted location.

The night provided many haunted events, with Marcy hitting paranormal paydirt with her pendulum session. She was able to get the name Isabel Sipah, who said she was a Native from the 1890s. She told the APPS group that she loved flowers and that irises had been her favorite. The APPS team

The haunted diner Foxy Roxy's. *Courtesy of the Adirondack Park Paranormal Society.*

heard thumps, footsteps and voices. One investigator, Brett, was also touched on the shoulder, and multiple team members witnessed a child ghost sitting at the top of the stairs with their hand on the railing. Shadow people were seen darting back and forth throughout the night, and one EVP in the attic caused a quick temperature drop, from 66° Fahrenheit to 59° Fahrenheit. The Adirondack Park Paranormal Society always goes through all its evidence with an eagle paranormal eye. Only the full agreement of the full team deems something paranormal, and the team members unanimously voted that Foxy Roxy's is 100 percent APPS-certified paranormal. One last note: in the APPS team's research post-investigation, they discovered that there was an Isabel Sipah who had lived in Potsdam in 1890. She had come from Lima, Peru, and was part of the Sequoia tribe.

BEST OF THE REST

The following is a list of additional haunted locations within the blue line of the Adirondacks. The Adirondacks are overstuffed with the paranormal and haunted locations; however, these are spots that have been deemed ghost infused. I encourage you to visit and see if the spirits paranormally meet and greet you.

Adirondack History Center Museum
Elizabethtown

The ghost of Henry De Bosnys walks the halls of this 1916 neoclassical former schoolhouse that now hosts history of the Adirondacks. Henry was hanged in 1883, and you can see his skull on display in the museum. His restless spirit has frightened visitors for decades. Staff and volunteers are always being frightened by Henry and other entities that roam the building and leave newspaper articles for the mortals to connect them to the other side.

The Strand Theater
Old Forge

Up on the screen, the movies are showing, the moviegoers have their peanuts, popcorn, candy and slushies, and they just might have a ghost in the seat next to them, enjoying the show. Fun and playful ghosts abound in the beautiful downtown theater. Built in 1923, the Strand hosts fun, love and ghosts. The owners, staff and moviegoers have interacted with spirits that love the movies as much as the living.

Barkeater Chocolates
North Creek

Visit the former family home that's now a chocolate factory, and you just might meet Miranda, the ghost who loves to turn up the thermostat. The former owners passed away in the building that now has unexplained voices, banging on walls and footsteps from the spirits.

Maxson House
Old Forge

One of the most haunted locations investigated in the annals of the Ghost Seekers of Central New York, this quant building on the main drag sells gifts and curiosities to tourists, yet the ghost of a little girl named Pumpkin plays with the teddy bears, taps on the child piano and calls out to the owners by name. Footsteps are heard there, and a large male entity haunts the building and likes to get up close to the ladies.

Landon Hill Bed and Breakfast
Chestertown

The beautiful haunted home was built in 1862 and has had many uses in its life, but most recently, it has housed slumbering guests who get more than a warm bed and tasty breakfast. Ghosts talk at all hours of the night, mirrors fall off the walls and televisions and other electronic devices turn on and off, even when they aren't plugged in. The ghosts of the Landon coexist peacefully with the travelers who are curious and brave enough to spend the night.

Riverview Cemetery
Old Forge

The ghost of Stephen Bazyliv walks the cemetery at night while on patrol. He was a veteran of the Great War (or World War I), in which he was wounded in the Battle of Verdun. He moved to Old Forge and fell in love with the area, and he later became a beloved citizen. He died in a tragic hunting accident, and his ghost is now seen along with mist that forms at the foot of his tombstone. The Riverview Cemetery is a small yet quaintly haunted and beautiful spot for the afterlife. Be sure to salute the ghost of the brave soldier.

Hummingbird Home
Plattsburgh

The former homestead had been a funeral home, and now, the leftover objects from the past have ghosts clinging to them. Visitors comment on the beauty of the home being back to its original luster; however, dentures, casket lifts and rosaries are among many leftover haunted objects. Get close to them if you dare.

Tony Harper's Pizza and Clam Shack
Old Forge

Live music on the upper deck, whiskey wings in the bar area and ghosts walking the building, bothering the waitstaff and fun-loving customers. The Harleys line up in the summer and the snowmobiles in the winter, but when you delve into the haunted bar area, the back bakery area and the sleeping quarters of the employees, there are spirits packed from top to bottom at Tony Harper's.

Pine Ridge Cemetery
Saranac Lake

The tiered cemetery in the middle of the town hosts ghosts and some of the most beautiful headstones in the Adirondack. You'll be drawn to the grave of Carl Lumholtz (1851–1922), the world-famous Norwegian scientist and explorer who was the first to analyze and write about life among Native people in his bestseller *Among Cannibals*. His spirit wanders Pine Ridge Cemetery as he explores for infinity in the afterlife.

The Tap Room
Raquette Lake

The Tap Room is a small, quaint corner pub that serves cold beverages and hosts ghosts within the bar and in the rooms above, where guests wake to voices, visions and all sorts of curious otherworldly spirits looking to join in the earthly fun. There's a female ghost in a flowered dress who acts as the paranormal caretaker. Stop in and have a ghostly good time.

Cedar Grove Cottages
Blue Mountain Lake

The last cottage on the left is home to the ghost of a young girl that has been seen by many. One witness described her as being eleven years old, with blond hair, wearing green pants with a white cardigan sweater. This all gives the impression that she's a contemporary spirit.

Fort Ticonderoga
Ticonderoga

Built in 1755, this fort took part in the French and Indian War and the Revolutionary War, and today, it hosts ghosts of the wandering type. The ghost sightings at the fort began in the mid-nineteenth century, when the spirit of a Native girl was spotted roaming the grounds. There's a spiritual sadness to the fort, as thousands died within its walls from disease. This national landmark has ghosts walking the halls; footsteps are heard, and mysterious paranormal lights pulsate. The ghosts of the sad and the brave live in the afterlife with honor.

The Union Depot
Saranac Lake

The depot has been certified haunted by the Adirondack Park Paranormal Society (APPS). Founder and lead investigator Damon Jacobs and his crack ghost team investigated the now-closed depot where spirits abound. The Union Depot sits next to the fomerly active railroad, and it was used long ago to bring people from around the United States afflicted with tuberculosis to the Adirondack Cottage Tuberculosis Sanitarium to be cured or have their suffering eased by the cool, crisp Adirondack air. Many would never leave alive, and their bodies were shipped back out on the train, back to their loved ones to be buried elsewhere, yet their spirits remained not only up at the sanitarium, but also at the Union Depot.

Jane McCrea House
Fort Edward

The legend of Jane McCrea is one of love, tragedy and death. Jane, twenty-five, was the daughter of a reverend and murdered at the hands of a Huron-Wendat warrior who was associated with the British army. Her death caused a rise in Patriot recruitment, as colonists could no longer believe in protection from the British. It's been said her death assisted in the swell of soldiers that ended up swaying the tide in the Battle of Saratoga. Cora's fiancé never married, and her tragedy inspired the character of the raven-haired beauty Cora in the *Last of the Mohicans*. Jane's home in Fort Edward is reported to be haunted, with many experiences documented by those who live there. The beautiful white home with green shutters is still occupied by locals, and the ghost of Jane still walks the halls, looking for her long-lost love.

Ohana's 1950s Diner
Tupper Lake

On the main drag through Tupper Lake, there is a 1950s-style diner that serves burgers, fries, milkshakes and ghosts. The interior has forty-five records adorning its walls, a jukebox and many locals and tourists filling the booths. Ohana's has long been haunted and is included in the New York State Haunted History Tour.

Wellscroft Lodge
Upper Jay

The summer retreat, built in 1903 by Wallis Smith and Jean Wells, hosts the ghost of the red lady. Many visitors have experienced her spectral visits near the main staircase, where her paranormal red dress flows as she stares out the front windows. Without warning, the ghosts will play music on the second floor. They don't charge, as money is not necessary in the afterlife.

GHOST GLOSSARY

There are many phrases and terms used in this book to describe ghosts, the equipment used to find them and the phenomenon of interacting with the dead. The following is a list that will educate you, fair reader, the exact meaning of these terms.

afterlife. Life after death.

angel. A spiritual being superior to earthbound humans in intelligence and power.

apparition. A ghost that gives the appearance of physical substance.

Bigfoot. An eight-foot-tall anthropoid hairy creature with foul breath and a skunk-like stench. Called Sasquatch by Native Americans. An elusive and possible paranormal interdimensional creature that appears throughout the Adirondacks and other parts of the United States.

clairvoyance. The ability to perceive matters beyond the range of ordinary perception.

cold spots. Haunted locations that have cool air that could be attributed to a ghost in close proximity.

conjure. To sumon the devil or a spirit by incantation or invocation. Practicing magical arts.

déjà vu. An unexpected sense of familiarity to a new person, object, place or experience.

demon. An evil spirit or dark supernatural being.

dowsing rods. Handheld metal rods that can be used to locate underground water sources or to communicate with the dead.

ectoplasm. A substance thought to be the manifestation of a ghost. Looks white and cloudy in appearance.

electronic voice phenomenon (EVP). When you capture a voice from the other side on a digital recording device or any device that captures voices. EVPs occur when you know there was no answer, but later on, you listen back and get a ghostly voice from the other side, either warning you, answering you or uttering nonsensical phrases. The theory is that the ghost voices have a frequency that cannot be heard by the human ear but can be captured on recording devices. These can be rather dramatic. A popular ghost EVP would be the famous paranormal line: "Get out!"

EMF detector. EMF meters measure fluctuations in electromagnet fields (or EM fields). These fields are the direct results of electrical appliances in homes, cellphones, power lines outside and even fluctuations in solar activity and weather. Beyond that, a primary theory in the paranormal world is that entities can manipulate these fields in their attempt to manifest themselves or interact with our world. The unit of measurement registered on an EMF meter is called milligauss. When using the EMF as a tracking device, look for fluctuations of 2.0 to 7.0, as this usually indicates the presence of a spirit. Anything higher or lower is normal and has a natural source.

empath. A person who can feel another person's emotions as their own. Having the ability to scan a person's energy for thoughts, feelings and past, present and future occurrences.

entity. Another term for a ghost.

ghost. A person's spirit and soul in the afterlife that appears to the living.

ghost lights, spirit lights, orbs. Spheres that are translucent, colored and can act intelligently. Sometimes, they have conical circles or faces inside. A partial manifestation of a ghost.

hag. An ugly, evil-looking woman or witch.

haunted/haunting. A place that shows significant paranormal activity. A place frequented by a ghost.

homunculus. A small fully formed human that is produced by alchemy and was popularized in the sixteenth century.

incubus. A male demon that seduces mortal woman, many times, while they are asleep.

intelligent haunt. When a ghost, spirit, shadow person or entity interacts with a mortal witness. An example would be if you saw the ghost of a soldier walking the grounds of Fort Ticonderoga, something is said and the ghost stops, looks, throws something or speaks or gestures. The ghost is responding and interacting with earthbound humans. This is the spirit acting independently and intelligently.

intuitive. The human brain tapping into the subconscious in order to provide guidance.

medium. A psychic who has fine-tuned their abilities in order to interface with the spirits in another dimension. They can hear and feel thoughts, voices and mental impressions.

mel meter. When you need to measure EMF and temperature, you need one instrument that gives you a wealth of information and plenty of options. This device offers both single-axis AC magnetic field measurement and real-time air temperature readings.

out-of-body. Relating to the feeling of hovering above or separating from your body and observing it from the outside.

paranormal. Anything outside of the realm of normality. This can include ghosts, UFOs, dimensional beings, cryptozoology and anything outside the realm of science and human understanding.

poltergeist. A ghost that makes noise and plays pranks on the living.

portal. A gateway from the earthly realm to the dimension of the dead.

possession. A person who is taken over by an interloping ghost.

psychic. Being able to perceive information that can include predicting the future, talking to the dead and being able to locate missing objects and people.

residual haunt. When a ghost appears at the same place and time and does the same thing over and over again. It's like a broken record that keeps repeating. In this realm, when we speak to these entities, they will not respond. The theory is that their deaths were so tragic that it left an imprint of spiritual energy that we can witness on replay for all eternity.

séance. A gathering of people to contact a loved one or a spirit. Popular in the nineteenth century's age of spiritualism.

shadow person. A ghost or being from another dimension or plane of existence who is all black in appearance—in the form of a shadow—yet moves intelligently.

soul. The essence of individual life that lies within all living human beings and separates on death to travel to the afterlife.

spirit. From the Latin word that means "that which breathes." Another term used to describe a ghost.

spirit box. A great tool for communicating with paranormal entities. It uses radio frequency sweeps to generate white noise, which theories suggest give some entities the energy they need to be heard. When this occurs, you will sometimes hear voices or sounds coming through the static in an attempt to communicate. You can get intelligent responses from the spirits using this device.

succubus. A female demon that seduces male humans, many times, while they are asleep.

BIBLIOGRAPHY

Adirondack Express, October 27, 2015.

Atlas Obscura. "Lake George Mystery Spot." www.atlasobscura.com.

Bartholomew, Paul, Robert Bartholomew, William Brann and Bruce Hallenbeck. *Monsters of the Northwoods*. Utica, NY: North Country Books, 1800.

Brandon, Craig. *Murder in the Adirondacks: An American Tragedy Revisited*. Utica, NY: North Country Books, 1986.

Dedam, Kim Smith. "Paranormal Team Confirms Spirits at Hotel Saranac." *Press-Republican*, October 31, 2015.

Encyclopedia Britannica. "Adirondack Mountains." January 7, 2019. www.britannica.com.

Goff, Susan Murphy, and Jessica Trombley. *History of the Stagecoach Inn at Elba, New York*. Lake Placid, NY: N.p., November 2019.

Goodsell Museum. "A Tribute to George & Jennie Goodsell." www.webbhistory.org.

Grow, Brittany. "The Woods Inn and the Van Auken's Inne Seem to Have an 'In' With Paranormal Guests."

Haunted History Trail of New York State. www.hauntedhistorytrail.com.

History of the Old Forge Hardware Store. www.oldforgehardware.com.

Merritt, Pamela. "Bigfoot in the Adirondacks." *Saranac Lake Newsletter*, n.d. www.saranaclake.com.

Nudi, Erin. "The Sagamore Named One of Top 10 Most Haunted Hotels in the U.S." www.lakegeorge.com.

Other Side TV. "Ghost Glossary of Paranormal Terms." www.theothersidetv.ca.

Rauch, Ned P. "A Fork in the Road." *Adirondack Life*, November 29, 2012. www.adirondacklifemag.com.

Stites, Karen A. "Murder Most Foul in the North Country: The Legend of Jane McCrea." *Sun Community News*, August 27, 2019.

Webster, Dennis, and Bernadette Peck. *Haunted Old Forge*. Charleston, SC: The History Press, 2016.

York, Michelle. "Century after Murder, American Tragedy Draws Crowd." *New York Times,* July 11, 2006.

Zambrano, Lynn. "What Is the Difference in Empath, Intuitive, Psychic, Medium, and Healer?" *Om Times*. www.omtimes.com.

ABOUT THE AUTHOR

Dennis Webster is the published author of books on ghosts, true crime and asylums. He's the founder, lead investigator, ghost hunter and paranormal investigator with the Fort Schuyler Paranormal Society. He's a paranormal advisor with the Adirondack Park Paranormal Society (APPS) and a former member of the Ghost Seekers of Central New York. He has danced with the realm of the dead, crossed the threshold to another dimension, done battle with the grim reaper, gotten intimate with a succubus during a seance and has survived it all to tell his story of the paranormal. He has a bachelor of science degree from Utica College and a master's of business administration degree (MBA) from State University of New York Polytechnic Institute. He can be contacted by mental telepathy or by email at denniswbstr@gmail.com.